# Moving Out:
## Practical Life Advice for
## Young Adults

SUZANNE KNEBES

ISBN: 1511630868
ISBN-13: 978-1511630863

# DISCLAIMER

This guide is intended as a general reference. Readers should use their own good judgment and common sense when applying advice to their personal situations. The author is not being compensated for any recommendations of products, name brands, or websites. Although every effort has been made to make the information it contains accurate, the author is not an expert or professional in any of the categories of the book including lawyer, doctor, psychologist, mechanic, or banker; therefore the advice should not be relied upon as professional advice but simply as the opinion of the author. The author and publisher claim no personal liability, either directly or indirectly, for the information presented within.

# DEDICATION

This book is dedicated to my children, Max and Melissa, who helped me to appreciate life by viewing it through their amazing eyes and to Tom, who makes every day so much fun.

*"Forgive yourself for not knowing what you didn't know*

*before you learned it."*

- *Maya Angelou*

# INTRODUCTION

The idea for this book came from remembering all of the phone calls I received from my grown kids after they had moved out of our home and into their first apartments.

They were smart kids with lots of common sense but situations arose that they had never come across before and they needed someone to confer with to make sure they didn't screw up.

As parents, our job is to prepare our kids for adulthood. We try, but sometimes we get busy and miss things. Sometimes we explain things but it simply doesn't stick. That's why I wrote this book. It's like a phone call to a parent. It attempts to answer the questions that will inevitably come up after entering that exciting life stage called 'adulthood'.

It isn't necessary to read this book cover to cover. It's meant to be a reference where readers can go directly to the chapter that deals with their current question or problem.

I hope this helps to give young adults the information they need to go confidently out on their own.

# CONTENTS

# ACKNOWLEDGMENTS

I'd like to offer a sincere thank you to my friends and family who helped me with this, my first self-published book. Thank you to my talented niece, Robin McDonagh, for the cover layout. She is my reliable go-to expert on everything graphic-design related. My appreciation goes out to Gil Loppnow and Dave Jones for their advice and expertise. Thanks to my niece, Shannon, for taking what precious free time she has while caring for her new baby girl to read every word and offer her thoughtful changes and additions. My kids were the inspiration for this book but they also offered their encouragement, input, suggestions, corrections, and editing skills, so thank you Max, Missy and Jenny. And thank you to my husband, Tom, not only for his constant love and support, but for his advice and knowledge of everything automotive.

*"Sometimes I think that the one thing I love the most about being an adult is the right to buy candy whenever and wherever I want."*

*- Ryan Gosling*

# 1 LEGALITIES

You're 18 and you are officially a legal adult. Yay. You've been waiting for this day for a long time. You get to make your own decisions now. Your parents can't boss you around anymore. You can date whomever you want, enlist in the armed services, have a beer (as long as you're 21, of course). It's all good, right?

Not so fast.

As a kid, your parents punished you when you did something wrong. But most likely your punishments were pretty mild, even if you didn't think so at the time.

Well, you're an adult now and you won't be getting grounded anymore. However, there will still be consequences when you screw up. Only now those consequences are a little more serious.

At 18, you can be held to a contract that you sign.

At 18, you can be sued.

At 18, you can be tried as an adult for a crime and go to jail.

This isn't meant to scare you but to impress upon you that along with the freedoms of adulthood come the responsibilities.

Have fun and enjoy this amazing time of your life but, along the way, follow the rules of the law and try to be a good tenant, neighbor, employee, and citizen.

*"Life is too complicated not to be orderly."*


*- Martha Stewart*


# 2 RENTING YOUR FIRST APARTMENT


Maybe you're in college and don't want to live in the dorms any more. Or you've been living in your parents' house but want your privacy and independence. Whatever the reason, you're ready for your first apartment.


Cost is going to determine the location and the size of your apartment. I'm assuming that you'll be paying your own rent or, at the very least, living on a budget. As a general rule, your rent shouldn't be more than one-third of your take-home pay. This may be difficult in high-rent areas (LA, NYC, Chicago, etc.) but do your best to follow that benchmark. You'll want some money left over for food, gas and fun, after all.

Factor in all the costs associated with the apartment. Are utilities included? If not, ask which ones you are responsible for and their average monthly costs. Are appliances included or will you have to provide them? Is there a washer and dryer in the apartment or in the building or will you have to take your laundry to a laundromat. Coin laundry machines can be expensive (save up those quarters) and time consuming.

Even though money is probably tight, don't sacrifice safety when choosing the location of your apartment. If you don't have a car, you'll need to feel safe walking to and from your home. How close to mass transit are you? If you have a car, does your apartment come with a parking spot? If not, is street parking readily available or will you constantly be hunting for an open spot and be at risk for amassing expensive parking tickets?

**Leases:**

All landlords are different, but you should expect to have two-months' worth of rent saved up before you get an apartment. You'll likely be asked to supply a security deposit that is equal to one month's rent PLUS the first month's rent. Some landlords even require first month's rent, last month's rent, AND a security deposit. If you have no credit history, they may ask that someone (such as a parent) co-sign your lease.

Often you'll be asked to sign a one-year lease. A lease protects both you and the landlord—you, by knowing your rent remains the same throughout the term of the lease and the landlord by knowing (s)he's guaranteed to have money coming in for the term of the lease. If it's not specified or if you don't re-sign after the year is up, the lease will usually revert to a month-to-month lease after the first year. Depending on the situation, that can be good or bad. Month-to-month leases give both you and the landlord flexibility—you to move out and the landlord to raise your rent. Base your decisions about leases on your particular situation.

A landlord may require references and a credit report. Be prepared with the names and phone numbers of people who will vouch for your character and your ability to pay the rent (current or past employers are ideal). Print off a copy of a recent credit report and take it with you so that each place where you submit an application doesn't ding your credit (more on that in the chapter on Budgeting).

**Utilities:**

So you have a new and cool apartment. You can't wait to start filling it up with furniture and making the space your own. There's one more step in between, though. You need to call the utility companies and put their services in your name or you'll be sitting in the dark in your new apartment freezing your butt off because you have no lights or heat. Utilities are things like electricity, gas, water/sewer and cable. Sometimes you may even be required to pay for trash or landscaping. Ask your landlord which ones you're responsible for and the names and numbers of the companies to deal with in your area. Ideally you want to call them *before* your move-in date to request that service start *on* your move-in date. If you have no credit or bad credit, they may ask you for a deposit before starting service. Cable is awesome but can end up being your most expensive utility bill if you go crazy with add-ons (cable, internet, phone, DVR, higher internet speeds, premium channels, extra cable boxes, etc.). Decide what you need before you call and what you can do without. Maybe you can go without internet service at all by using public internet hotspots (libraries, Starbucks, Panera, etc.). Maybe *all* you need is internet service and then you can stream movies and TV shows (maybe you could use your parents' Netflix, Amazon Prime password, and HBO Go accounts!).

**Renter's Insurance:**

Your lease may require you to get renter's insurance. Even if it doesn't, you should consider it. You may be thinking, "Most of my stuff isn't good enough to be worth stealing." But renter's insurance doesn't just cover your stuff. It covers the interior of your apartment and also you if you are sued.

Let's say you want to take a bath so you turn on the water in the tub. But it takes a while to fill up so you lie down on your bed to wait and . . . . . you promptly fall asleep. You're awakened to angry knocks on your door. The old lady whose apartment is right below yours is yelling that water is coming through her ceiling and she's mad as hell. Next, the landlord is telling you that you are liable for all the repairs to both your apartment and the old lady's downstairs. THAT's why you should get renter's insurance.

Renter's insurance also provides personal liability coverage, meaning, it protects you if someone sues you. Maybe you injured someone while playing football in the park (you forgot it was 'tag' not 'tackle') or your dog nipped at the mailman. With renter's insurance, you're covered.

Note that most insurers now offer computer insurance as an add-on item. While your basic policy will cover theft, fire, and vandalism, this extra rider covers dropping your computer or spilling on it. Ask whether it will pay for actual cash value or replacement value. Cash value reimburses you for what something is worth today (used price) while replacement value covers the cost of buying a brand new version of your item.

The best way to save money on renter's insurance is to use the same insurance company that you use for your car insurance. You can save a bundle by bundling.

**Furnishings:**

The other major cost when you get your first apartment is furnishings. Maybe you've staked a claim to your family's basement couch and television but don't forget you also need dishes, silverware, cookware, sheets, blankets, pillows, and towels. You may also want blinds or curtains for privacy, a shower curtain to keep the bathroom floor dry and maybe a couple of pictures on the wall.

If you're one of the oldest of the kids in your family, your parents or grandparents may have some items they're willing to part with (and an excuse for them to go out and get brand-new stuff for their own homes). Take them. I know, they're probably not your style. But remember that they are FREE and your budget is going to be stretched with so many things that you need for this first apartment that it might be the difference between having a bed and sleeping on a borrowed, blow-up mattress.

If you're like me and you're the number-five son or daughter and all of the family hand-me-downs have already been handed out, then it's time to start looking for bargains. Visit rummage or garage sales in your area and be prepared to dicker. Offer half their asking price, throw in a sob story about being young and poor and see how low they'll go. Craigslist is a great place to get used furniture for a fraction of its original price, but be ready to pay cash and to pick it up yourself. (Hint: first check out the "FREE" section on Craigslist). Home Goods is a great discount store for dishes, silverware, bedding and even some furniture or rugs. IKEA has some modern and innovative stuff at incredibly-low prices.

Not all apartments come with appliances. Sometimes you'll be required to supply your own refrigerator and stove. Be sure to shop around for second-hand, gently-used options.

If you don't have a good friend with a pick-up truck to get your stuff over to your new apartment, you can always rent a U-Haul for the day. Their daily rates are inexpensive but know that they tack on a mileage fee. Home Depot rents trucks or vans by the hour. If you ask your friends to help you move, be a sport and treat them to sandwiches and drinks afterward as a thank you.

**Pets:**

Before you rush out and buy that puppy that you've always wanted but your parents wouldn't allow you to have, consider this: finding an apartment that allows pets cuts down your options by 65% (according to MyApartmentMap, a company that compiles nationwide stats on rentals).[i] If a rental does allow pets, many times they will require an additional pet deposit. Also know that having a pet may add to your rental insurance costs and that there are several breeds of dogs that insurance companies won't cover at all.

Along with the financial responsibilities of owning a pet (food, vet, etc) are the limitations to your freedom. Having a pet may mean forgoing an outing or a vacation if you can't find someone to care for it in your absence. You may have to come home right after work to let the dog out instead of going to the gym or out for drinks with your co-workers.

For the record, I'm not telling you to get rid of a beloved pet—I'm an animal lover too. I simply want you to be aware of issues you may not have considered so that you can factor them into your decision. FYI—there is no such thing as window shopping for a puppy. You might say you're just going to go look at them, but you know as well as I do that you'll be coming home with the first one that licks your face and gives you its best sad, puppy eyes.

**Roommates:**

To keep costs down or simply for fun and security, you may choose to have a roommate or two (or more). I recommend you discuss a few things ahead of time and maybe even come up with a Roommate Agreement *before* you move in together. It will clarify expectations and help to ensure that your friendship(s) survives the roommate-ship.

Some topics for discussion might include:

> *Chores (who does what, when, and how often):* Initiate a cleaning schedule for common areas to avoid arguments about who is always cleaning up after the

other(s). Be considerate and clean up after yourself. Wipe down the bathroom sink and counter when you're done with your morning routine. Wash your own dishes after each meal (and rinsing them but leaving them in the sink doesn't count).

*Groceries:* Establish boundaries/rules for eating each other's food. Divide the fridge/cabinets and if you have to 'borrow' from your roommate's stash, make sure you replace or repay. There's nothing more irritating than looking forward to those chocolate chip cookies that you splurged on and finding an empty shelf instead.

*Utilities:* Utilities are usually registered in just one roommate's name making that person ultimately responsible for the bill (or the non-payment of the bill). Having your name on the bill can help you to establish credit, but it could end up harming your credit if the bill goes unpaid.

*Guests:* Discuss rules on overnight guests. How often is it appropriate for a significant other to spend the night? When does an overnight guest become a freeloader—living in your apartment, dirtying the bathroom, and eating the food but not paying their fair share of rent and utilities? Trust me, it'll come up.

*Pets:* Do you have a pet? Do you want a pet? Are you allergic to animals? Does the lease allow pets? Have the discussion before your roommate comes home with that adorable kitten from the Humane Society that you can't find in your heart to send away.

*Schedules:* Are you a morning person who gets up at 7:00 and clanks around in the kitchen or maybe a night owl who blasts the TV into the wee hours? Roommates don't necessarily have to be on the same schedule. In fact, sometimes opposite schedules are ideal because each gets some privacy and the use of the bathroom when they need it. Most schedule problems can be avoided just by having consideration for each other.

## Cleaning:

Here's a topic that many of you are going to skip. For those of you who don't, thank you from the bottom of my Monica-ish heart. (I write with the hope that the 'Friends' reference is still relatable.) Here's my advice—keep your home organized and neat. Not only is your home a reflection of you, but it can alter your mood and affect your well being. A dirty, disorganized home can make your life feel dirty and disorganized. And it won't impress any dates that you bring home either. (Again I'll use the 'Friends' reference—the one where Ross is dating a really hot chick but goes to her house and finds a disgusting pigsty. No degree of hotness can overcome a messy, sticky, disgusting apartment.)

Keeping a neat home is easier than you may think. First, everything should have a logical place: clothes in drawers or closets or hampers, papers on a desk (ideally in piles or files such as 'to-do/to-pay' and 'paid') or in a drawer or file cabinet, dishes and food in the kitchen. Having a logical place for things also helps you to locate them even if you can't remember where you put something. Where SHOULD it be? Finally, the more you deal with clutter on a daily basis, the easier the weekly cleaning is.

Now the bad news—you actually have to *buy* cleaning supplies with your own money. And all this time you thought they just appeared magically under the sink. Basic cleaning supplies to have on hand include: dish soap, all purpose cleaner, toilet bowl cleaner, glass cleaner, bucket, toilet brush, plunger (now there's something you want to have BEFORE you need it!), broom/mop/Swiffer and a vacuum cleaner if you have carpeting. (You can usually buy used vacs very reasonably at garage sales or on Craigslist.) There are some very good non-toxic cleaning supplies on the market that do the job nicely without putting unneeded chemicals into your home and our water/waste systems. Or make your own and save money in the process— http://www.livingwellspendingless.com/2013/03/13/green-thrifty-cleaning-products/.

Once a week (okay, you can stretch it to two weeks if you're really busy) you should give your apartment a good cleaning. Here's the process in 5 easy steps:

1. Wipe all counters in the kitchen and bathroom(s). That means moving things and wiping underneath. Wipe out the inside of the microwave. Wipe down the frig and the stovetop. Scrub the sinks.

2. Dust all surfaces (tables, shelves, dressers, desks) with a soft rag or Swiffer Duster. Don't forget the tops of pictures, the rungs of the chairs, lamps— anything with a flat surface that can collect dust.

3. Clean the toilet using a toilet bowl cleaner and toilet brush. Then take a rag and wipe the lid, the top and bottom of the seat, the rim (boys, do a courtesy wipe of the rim and floor whenever you miss or dribble) and the outside of the bowl, in that order to avoid spreading germs.

4. Spray the tub with an all-purpose cleaner and rinse. Wipe down all the ledges around the tub. Use an anti-mold product on any black spots that start to develop. If you catch them early, they'll simply rinse away; otherwise you'll have to scrub with a brush. If your tub has glass sliding doors, they may acquire a lime/calcium build-up due to hard water. To avoid it, use a squeegee after every shower. To treat it, use a hard-water remover such as Lime A-Way.

5. Sweep/mop/vacuum all floors. I'm a huge fan of Swiffers for floors (dry first, then wet). Steam mops are great too.

It won't take long to clean your whole apartment and it'll do wonders for your mood (and the bottoms of your socks).

**Laundry:**

Have a hamper or laundry basket within easy reach of your closet or dresser. You're more likely to put your dirty clothes in the laundry basket if it's in tossing range from where you change your clothes. I'm a big believer in hooks for reducing the amount of laundry you have. Hooks hold those in-between clothes—clothes that you've worn for half the day but that aren't ready for the hamper.

On washday, simply sort your dirty clothes into two piles--- dark and light. Wash your darks in cold water and your lights in warm or hot water. In addition to laundry detergent, I throw a scoop of all-color bleach (such as Oxi Clean) into the washing machine tub as it is filling and let it dissolve before I add the clothes. It helps keep my whites from going gray and it helps get rid of stains.

Read laundry labels before just throwing everything into the dryer or you could be handing your new wool sweater down to your little sister or brother. Make an effort to fold your clothes while they are still warm from the dryer. Most clothes these days come through the wash and dry process wrinkle-free; it's only the sitting in the dryer wadded up in a ball for hours that puts the wrinkles into them. When I'm tight on time and can't fold immediately, I at least pull items out of the dryer and lay them flat until I have the time to do a proper folding. For the occasions when you just can't be there when the dryer buzzer goes off, simply turn the dryer on for five minutes and fluff everything back up. Your clothes won't be as pristine as if you'd dealt with them the first time the dryer buzzed, but it'll help. If you keep some hangers near the dryer, you can hang up your shirts as they come out of the dryer and save yourself from having to iron them. And one more thing about dryers—yes, you have to remove the lint EVERY time you do a load. For one, lint clogs the screen so that the cycle takes longer to dry your items, but more importantly, a build-up of lint in your dryer can cause a fire. (Another reason you need renter's insurance!)

I try and minimize the number of clothes I take to the dry cleaner. Dry cleaners are expensive, and it's getting more so because of increased regulations about how they dispose of their chemicals. I only use a dry cleaner for clothes that say 'dry cleaning only' or for fancy stuff such as wedding-worthy clothing or important business attire. If you're required to wear a dress shirt to work everyday, consider buying wrinkle-free shirts. Or else you could consider a laundry service for your shirts. For some reason, that is one service that has remained reasonable; a professionally-ironed dress shirt makes a good impression every time. The reason I qualify this as a guy's option is that women's shirts may cost more to have laundered than men's. It was explained to me that it is because automated machinery is set up for men's shirts, not women's, and so women's ironing must be done mostly by hand.

If you decide your shirts need a touch up with the iron, here is a quick tutorial on how to iron a shirt. I received my ironing lessons from my grandmother-in-law, a cool old German lady who rivaled professionals with her ironing skills. I don't think I ever achieved her perfection but I can produce a respectable shirt when I need to. Start with a hot iron—use the highest setting when ironing cotton—and put some distilled water in it for creating steam.

1.  First do the collar, iron it flat.
2.  Next do the yolk (the panel across the back just under the collar).
3.  Move on to the sleeves—both sides of each one. Don't forget to iron the cuffs.
4.  Lastly, do the body of the shirt, starting with, let's say, the right, front panel and working your way around the back and finally to the left, front panel.

When you come upon a stubborn wrinkle, give it a spritz of steam (or you can leave the steam function on the entire time). Make a point to get the tip of the iron into all of the corners, up against all the seams, and in between and around any buttons. That's the secret of ironing. It's kind of like painting a wall—anyone can run a paintbrush or roller over the large expanses of a wall; the skill and attention to detail shows around the edges.

Here's a cheater's tip for those times when don't have time to wash or iron properly: spritz the clothing item with water (ideally with a spray bottle but the finger-flicking method will suffice) and then with Febreeze, and toss it in the dryer for ten minutes. Voila, you have a faux-clean and faux-ironed shirt for work or an impromptu date.

Make an effort to wash your sheets every week, if possible. I wash my towels on the same day to keep myself on a schedule. Towels can be used more than once before washing as long as you hang them up to dry properly between uses.

**Guests:**

Having guests in your home requires a balance between making them feel special and making them feel relaxed, as if it's their own home. I like to offer guests their first refreshment and then show them around the kitchen and invite them to help themselves from then on. If you know your guests well, try and have some of their favorites on hand.

Overnight guests can be tricky when you have a small apartment. Tell guests ahead of time what type of sleeping accommodations you can offer (bed, couch, blow-up mattress, floor?), and then they can decide whether or not to book a hotel instead. You are not obligated to give up your bed or bedroom for guests; however, you should at least offer them clean sheets, a pillow with a clean pillowcase, and blankets appropriate for the temperature of the apartment.

Most likely you'll be sharing your bathroom with your guests (unless your apartment has more than one). Make an effort to clean the bathroom before they arrive and offer them a clean towel to use during their stay. A nightlight is a nice touch so that guests can find the bathroom in the middle of the night.

It is totally reasonable to expect to maintain some areas of privacy when you have guests. Your bedroom is your private space and guests should not enter it without an invitation. Your desk, computer and papers are for your eyes only unless you've given your guest permission to view or use them.

*"Don't tell me where your priorities are. Show me where you spend your money and I'll tell you what they are."*

*- James W. Frick*

# 3 BUDGETING

A budget is a simple thing to make but a difficult thing to adhere to. It seems that the more money we make, the more we find to spend it on—there never seems to be enough.

So, here's a tip that will serve you throughout your entire life, if you can stick to it. **PAY YOURSELF FIRST. Save 10% of your income before you pay anyone else.** If you can do this throughout your life, you will never have to worry about money. It's called Living Beneath Your Means and almost nobody does it.

There are several ways to make a budget (and stick with it). You can use one of many phone or computer apps available (HomeBudget, Spendbook, Wally, Dollarbird, or Mint to name just a few). They will help you to correctly categorize your expenses and oftentimes also track them. Or you can get a broader overview of your monthly financials with this more informal approach. Take a piece of paper and put your current income on top. (Here's where, ideally, you deduct 10% to put into savings.) Next list your fixed expenses—things that are the same every month like rent, car payment, insurance, utilities, student loan, etc. Subtract your fixed expenses from your income. Next subtract your best guess of variable expenses like groceries, eating out, gas, and clothes.

No matter which method you use to keep track of your money, hopefully there's something left after you subtract your expenses from your income. If so, that's for all those things that you want but don't really need—your discretionary income. Now you can go shopping for those cool sunglasses or have that dinner out at your favorite restaurant. If there's nothing left, stay home with a library book, go for a hike, take that free yoga class in the park, or find some other healthy and free activity. Whatever you do, don't keep spending by using the credit card! Which brings us to the next subject . . . .

## Credit Cards:

In a nutshell: you should have one; you should not keep a balance on one.

Credit card companies make their money when you keep a balance on your card. Every month you get a bill that asks for a small minimum payment that, if you always only pay the minimum, ensures that the credit card company will make lots of money off of you forever.

So, pay off your credit cards every month and never, ever pay them late—not even by one day. Unlike your utility bill or a loan from your parents, if you're one day late with a credit card payment, you'll get zapped with a big ol' late fee. (Note, as soon as you realize your payment is late, call your credit card company, make the payment, and apologize. If it is a rare late payment, they may reverse the late-fee charges for you. But don't expect this to work more than once or twice.) If you're late a lot, not only will your interest rate on that card go up, but your card may be canceled so that you can't use it anymore. Don't think that gets you off the hook, though. You'll still owe the balance on the card (which will keep getting bigger because of the higher interest rate) and it'll be hard to get another card because your irresponsible behavior will have been reported to all of the credit agencies.

One way to avoid getting into trouble with credit card debt is to use your debit card instead of a credit card. Debit cards work the same as credit cards except the money comes right out of your checking account. To use it like a credit card, simply answer "credit" when the clerk asks you "debit or credit". You won't have to enter your pin number but it will still come out of your checking account.

You must never give anyone your pin and no one should ever ask you for it—not your bank, not a store clerk, and certainly not anyone contacting you by phone or email. Be safe when using your credit or debit cards online—always look for a secure transaction symbol before trusting a site with your information and always close the browser after you log out. If your card is lost or stolen, report it right away.[ii]

Try not to use your credit card for cash advances. The interest rate for a cash advance is much higher than the regular credit card interest rate plus there could be an additional fee. If you must take a cash advance off of your credit card, pay it back in full as soon as possible.

Which credit card company should you go with? That depends on what's important to you and how you plan on using your card. If you usually keep a balance, then a low interest rate is desirable. If you pay off your card each month (mostly) then maybe you want a card with perks like cash back or gifts or air miles. Go to a site like cardhub.com or nerdwallet.com to find the right card for you. Or apply for one at your bank if they offer a card that can be tied to your checking account. Shop around and always take interest rates and yearly fees into consideration.

**Checking Accounts:**

Everyone should have a checking account and establish a relationship with a bank or a savings and loan. A checking account gives you a safe place to deposit your paychecks. Most banks also have Bill Pay options that allow you to pay your bills online, saving you stamps and checks.

So, pick a bank that is near you and that has free checking. Open an account (you'll need a minimal amount, say $100 or so) and order checks. If you can, open a savings account at the same time. Use that savings account as the place to pay yourself first—10% if you can swing it. Connect the two accounts and designate your savings account as a backup to your checking account in case you accidentally overdraw your checking account. It'll save you from paying large overdraft fees.

If your employer offers you direct deposit, take it. That way your money is available to you the same day you get paid—no waiting and no overdrafts if you can't get to the bank on payday to cash your check.

You can manage your account online—either on your smart phone or on your computer. Track your balance by viewing it online or keep a detailed checkbook and balance it every month. (Don't forget to record any transactions you make with your debit card—think of it as writing a virtual check.) Banking mistakes are few and far between, but they do occasionally happen, so I still like to balance my checkbook. Call me a control freak.

If you are a control freak too, here's a quick tutorial on how to balance your checkbook. It isn't hard. Take your monthly statement from the bank and compare it to your checkbook.

1.  First, go the deposit section of the statement. For every deposit listed on the statement, find the same transaction in your checkbook and put a checkmark after it. (Note: if a deposit is listed on the statement but you forgot to record it in your checkbook, simply do it now, along with a check mark after it.) Get out your calculator and add up the deposits listed in your checkbook that don't have a checkmark after them (they would have occurred on or after the date on the statement). Now add that amount to the 'Ending Balance' on your statement.

2.  Next, go to the 'Checks Paid' and the 'Electronic Payments' sections on the statement and do the same thing—match each entry to one in your checkbook and put a checkmark after it. (Once again, if you forgot to enter a check or debit or a cash withdrawal, record it in your checkbook now

and put a check mark after it.) Add up any unchecked checks/debit entries and subtract that total from the 'Ending Balance' on your statement.

3. Here's a good time to add to your checkbook any interest the bank has paid you and subtract any fees that they have charged you and that you probably didn't know about until you got your statement. You now have your final checkbook balance.

4. Compare the new 'ending balance' on your statement (the statement's final number plus unchecked deposits from Step 1 and unchecked debits from Step 2) to your new checkbook balance. If it doesn't match and you're a control-freak like me, you'll recheck every number until they reconcile. It'll drive you crazy until you find the missing entry or the addition/subtraction mistake. Or . . . if you're not a control freak, simply adjust your checkbook and chalk it up to being one of the great mysteries of the universe.

Whatever you do, whether you monitor your checkbook by keeping good records and balancing it or you simply check it online, try never to overdraw your bank account. Overdraft fees can be steep--$35 or more. But mistakes happen, especially when budgets are tight. If you are overdrawn, remedy the situation as soon as possible. It won't affect your credit rating unless you ignore the situation and the bank is forced to turn it over to collection.[iii]

**Credit Scores:**

If you have ever applied for a credit card, taken out a loan or opened a bank account, you have a credit score. Creditors, landlords, and even employers may use your credit score as a tool to determine your financial reliability. A good credit score can get you a lower interest rate on your car loan (or mortgage). A bad credit score can cost you the car or the apartment you want. Therefore, it is in your best interest to monitor your credit score and to strive to improve it.

Your credit score is NOT based on your age or your income or even how much money you have in the bank. It is based on how much debt you have, whether or not you are trying to take on too much debt, and your reliability and timeliness in paying your debts.

Taking on some debt and establishing credit is important. A person with no credit cards might be considered a higher risk than someone who has managed their credit cards responsibly. To show that you are responsible, you must be zealous in paying your bills on time—especially bills involving banks or credit cards where being even one day late can trigger a fine and affect your score.

Other tips for improving your score include keeping your credit balances low relative to the available credit on the card and always making more than the minimum payment every month. Don't open too many accounts (I know, the perks that go with a Kohls, Macy's, Banana Republic, or Gap card are very tempting) especially over a short period of time or if you have a short credit history, and don't move balances from one account to another. Older credit card relationships are valued while opening new credit reduces your score.[iv]

If you have some problems with debt and it has affected your credit score, don't despair. Simply take control of the situation by going through your credit report (you are entitled to one free credit report every year plus a free one any time you have been turned down for credit) and correcting any errors on it. Next, institute responsible practices such as paying bills on time and reducing your debt. Older credit problems count for less as time goes on; recent good payment patterns are looked at favorably and will raise your score with time.

**Taxes:**

Most people I know dread tax time. You can minimize hassles by being aware of the forms and information that you'll need to do your taxes and then by keeping everything together in one place (and I don't mean the trash can). I keep a folder marked 'TAXES' on my desk.

The envelopes will start arriving in January from employers, banks, and investment companies containing forms with names like W-2, 1098, or 1099. Put these in your tax folder. If you've made any donations throughout the year, get receipts and put them in your tax folder too. Note that if you live in a state that has no state income tax (FL, NV, TX, WA, TN, NH, AK, SD, WY), you are allowed to deduct the sales taxes you paid throughout the year. There is a standard deduction for it, but if you've made a large purchase sometime during the year (a car, for example), you might benefit from itemizing.

You will have to file both a federal income tax form and a state income tax form (unless you live in one of the states without an income tax listed above in which case you'll just file a federal form) on or before April 15th every year. You can do your own taxes or you can use a tax preparer. If you do your own, you can either download the forms from irs.gov (for your federal tax form) and your home state's website (for your state form) or you can use tax preparation software such as TurboTax or HR Block Tax Software. Using a professional tax preparer may cost a bit more, but could save you money in the long run if they are able to point out deductions you missed.

Whether or not you owe money at tax time or get a tax refund will depend on a combination of how many exemptions you claimed on your W-4 at work, the state you live in, how much money you make (which tax bracket you're in), and how many deductions you are eligible for.

To reduce the chance that you'll owe money when tax time rolls around, claim zero exemptions on the W-4 that you fill out at work. (Note, every employee is required to fill out a W-4 when they are hired so that the employer can withhold the correct income taxes from the employee's paycheck. You may fill out a new W-4 whenever your situation changes, i.e. if you get married or have a child.) Every person is entitled to one exemption, plus an exemption for a spouse and each child under 18 that they support. Claiming fewer exemptions than you're entitled to ensures that your employer takes more than enough taxes out of every paycheck so that when you file your year-end taxes, ideally you'll get a refund rather than owe money.

On the other hand, you may prefer to pay only the taxes you owe, comfortable in the knowledge that you've saved enough to make up for any shortfalls. If that's the case, claim the exemptions you're entitled to and even up with the government at tax time.

Try not to wait until the last minute to do your taxes. If you're using a professional tax preparer, allow them days, or better yet weeks, to do their work. Starting early allows enough time to find those inevitable missing or misplaced documents or to get copies if the originals can't be found. If you are expecting a refund, it is in your best interest to submit early. If you owe money, you can simply wait until April 15th to submit your tax form and payment.

## Saving/Investing/Compounding:

Here's a tidbit I wish I had paid more attention to in my 20's: start saving and investing and compounding your earnings NOW! Take some of that 10% (or whatever amount you have managed to save) and invest it. Whatever interest or dividends it earns, invest that too. It's called compounding and it is the secret to exponentially increasing your wealth no matter how little you start with.

Here's an example of the power of compounding over time courtesy of Stansberry Research. A fictional 19-year old started putting $2,000/year into an IRA (at an average growth rate of 10%--7% interest plus growth) until he was 26 years old. At that point, he stopped adding to the fund and simply forgot about it. His best friend waited until he was 26 to start his IRA (he bought a car instead and spent his money taking girls out on dates) but then added $2,000 to it faithfully every year until he was 65 (at the same assumed growth rate). Which one do you think had more money at 65? Unbelievably, it's the one who started at 18 and only made 7 payments! Even though he only invested $14,000 total ($2,000/year times 7 years), his investment at age 65 was worth $930, 641. His friend invested $80,000 ($2,000/year for 40 years) and ended up at age 65 with $893,704. That's the power of compounding and starting early.[v]

There are several ways/places to invest your money. You can participate in your company 401K program or SEP (simplified employee pension) if one is offered. If the company offers any kind of matching, you should definitely participate—it's free money! You can also open your own IRA either through your bank, mutual fund company or through an investment firm.

## Money Wasters:

Here are a couple of very unnecessary ways to waste your money. I call the category, 'you might as well just light a match to it'.

*Overdraft or over-limit fees.* These are fees that the banks and credit card companies charge when you overdraw your checking account, exceed the limit on your credit card, or make a late payment on your credit card. Fees range from $35-$50 for each incident. In this day and age when you can access your accounts on your phone or on your computer, there is no reason not to know when your account is running low or when your payment is due. Sign up for alerts on all of your banking and credit card accounts and you will get a text or email when a payment is due or when an account has less than $100 in it.

*Parking, speeding, or any kind of traffic ticket.* It happens to all of us. We approach our parked car and see the dreaded paper tucked under our windshield wiper and flapping in the wind. Damn, a parking ticket. Then we search for the street sign we missed that would have told us it was a 20-minute parking slot or that no parking is allowed on Thursdays for street cleaning. To minimize wasting money on parking tickets, check for a sign whenever you park, keep a roll of quarters in your car for meters, set the alarm on your phone to warn you when you have 10 minutes left on your allotted time or meter, and be extra suspicious when you're the only car parked on one side of the street. To avoid speeding tickets . . . . don't speed. Avoiding any other traffic ticket (red light, pedestrian crossing, etc.) means you need to keep your attention on your driving instead of on your phone, on your food, on your reflection in the mirror, or on the passengers in your car.

*"Car sickness is the feeling you get when the monthly payment is due."*


*- Unknown*




# 4 CARS


Most of us dream about the cool cars we want to drive and own. When it comes to cars, we all tend to want more car than we can afford. We see the ads for new cars on TV and we want all the latest extras like Bluetooth, navigation, and keyless entry. Plus they come in such awesome colors.


Now comes the reality. Cars are expensive—probably your biggest expense after rent—so you'll need to be smart about which one you buy. Ideally, you want the coolest car that you can afford that is still safe, reliable, and that will retain the most value when it is time to sell it.

Different cars appeal to people for different reasons. My daughter loves her Mazda 3 because of the size and style. Subarus have all-wheel drive and might appeal to people who drive in the mountains or in snow. New BMWs are a blast to drive and come with free maintenance for the first four years or 50,000 miles—a great feature (and one we've taken advantage of several times). Camaros and Mustangs are affordable performance cars. Find the car that best matches your needs, your taste, and your budget.

Two car manufacturers that have great reputations for dependability, low maintenance costs, and for retaining their value are: Toyota and Honda. That's not to say that other cars are not desirable, but only that Toyota and Honda get high ratings in all three of the above-mentioned categories.

**To Buy or Lease:**

So here are your options:

1) You can take the money you have saved ($3,000? $5,000? have you saved anything?) and look for a used car that you can pay cash for. It may be a decade old or have a few dings or scrapes, but it'll be yours and you won't have any car payments for as long as you own it. If you go this route, it's important to buy a car that has a good reputation for reliability, meaning low maintenance costs. Try to steer clear of high-end used cars that have lots of bells and whistles. Those bells and whistles are

cool but they can be very expensive to fix. Our son learned that lesson the hard way. He fell in love with a 10-year old loaded Audi Allroad with air suspension. It was a very cool car but his repair bills in the first two years exceeded what he paid for the car originally.

2) Or . . . you can buy a new, almost-new, or certified-used car. Use the money you've saved as a down payment and apply for a car loan. You may be able to get a loan through a dealership, your own bank, or another source. Check for student or new-graduate deals or discounts. See if any of the dealerships near you are offering 0% interest or a low interest rate. Remember that the bigger your down payment, the lower your monthly payment—and vice versa.

3) The last option is to lease a car. Leasing allows you to get more car for your money (which is great) but at the end of the lease, you have nothing—you don't own a car that you can sell or trade on another vehicle (which is not so great). Lease terms can range from two to six years but, in my opinion, the sweet spot for a lease is three years because it is at that point that the car starts to need repairs and to depreciate faster. Leases come with mileage allowances (typically 10,000/, 12,000/, or 15,000/miles per year). When leasing, I like to plan for more mileage than I think I'll need—it's cheaper to add it on the front end in the form of a higher monthly payment than it is to pay per mile at the end of the lease if you go over your allowance. Read the fine print before signing a lease so that you're clear about possible extra charges at turn-in. You may be charged for 'excessive wear and tear'—dents or deep

scratches, cracks in windows, or torn upholstery. Some companies have a disposition fee or turn-in fee. Often they will waive it if you lease another car from them. I call it a 'failed-to-be-loyal fee' and consider it excessive, but that's just my opinion. Getting out of a lease early can be very expensive, so make sure you are willing and able to keep the car for the entire lease period. Our daughter leases her car. It allows her to have a reliable, safe car for about $200/month with no worries about expensive repair bills.

Note about leasing—due to the fact that lease prices depend so much on the residual value of the car at the end of the lease period, you may be able to lease a premium car at a comparable rate to a basic car. Also know that leases can be negotiated the same way a car purchase can. Comparison shop for deals and don't fall for the oft-used ploy that the deal you're being offered is only good for that day. If you are not allowed to go home and sleep on a large-purchase decision such as a car, then you don't want to deal with that salesman or dealership.

If you're still unsure whether to buy or lease, here's a suggestion: find a car you're interested in, sit down with a salesperson and agree on a purchase price for the car. (Car salesmen hate to do this but ask anyway.) Then ask them to figure the payments two ways: as a purchase and also as a lease (and make sure that they include taxes and registration costs in the final quotes). Tell them how much you are willing to put down on the vehicle (you don't always *have* to put money down but it lowers your monthly payments, helps you to get a better interest rate on your loan/lease, and reduces the chances of becoming upside down in your car—that is, owing more than it's worth). Then compare the deals. If buying, note the length of the term and the interest rate. If leasing, note the length of the lease and the yearly mileage allowed. In most cases, the lease will have a lower monthly cost because the amount financed is only a few year's worth of the value of the car (the lease term) whereas the amount financed on a loan is for the entire purchase price of the car. Remember, though, that at the end of the lease, you have nothing whereas at the end of the loan, you have a paid-off car with some value.

In case you haven't noticed, I've been going on the assumption that you'll purchase or lease your car through a dealership. Buying from a reputable dealership has a few advantages for an inexperienced buyer. First, the dealership will handle the paperwork, financing, and registration. Secondly, you have a place you can go if you have a problem with the car. Reputations are important to local businesses, so they are unlikely to purposely cheat you or stick you with a lemon car.

With all of that said, buying from an individual can be a cheaper way to go. If you find a car online that you love and that is in your price range, I recommend taking your best gearhead-friend with you when you go to look at the car. Watch out for the following:

1.  Drive the car and listen for any sounds that aren't the nice purr of a smooth-running engine. If the car doesn't shift smoothly between gears, there could be a problem with the transmission. Transmissions are expensive to fix or replace so you may want to walk away.

2.  There shouldn't be any smoke coming out of the exhaust on start-up or while it's running and don't believe anyone that tells you that it's not a big deal if there is. It's NOT normal and it IS a big, expensive deal.

3.  The same goes for leaks of any kind of fluid (other than water) on the ground underneath the car. Walk away and do not look back.

4.  Turn on the air conditioner to make sure it works. If they say it just needs to be recharged, again, walk away. If the issue was that simple, they would have fixed it themselves before listing the car.

5.  Look at the tread on the tires to make sure the tires don't need replacing—a new set of tires will cost in the range of $600-$800. Uneven tire wear (more wear on either the inside or the outside of front tires) can be an indication of suspension, shocks, or alignment problems.

6.  Ask the seller for the maintenance records on the car. Someone who has been diligent about oil changes and upkeep should have the records to prove it.

7.  Run a CARFAX (www.carfax.com) on the car to see if it has been in any accidents or has had major repairs that the seller isn't disclosing. (After Hurricane Katrina, used cars came on the market

that had been flooded and unscrupulous sellers weren't fessing up. A CARFAX would have, in most cases, enlightened any buyer savvy enough to check.) All you need to run the CARFAX is the VIN number of the car, which can be found on the driver's side of the dashboard.

Remember the old adage, Buyer Beware. No one can guarantee that a used car won't have problems, but you can reduce the chances by doing your due diligence.

No matter where you buy your car, especially if you are buying a used car, you'll want to make sure that you are paying a fair price for the car. You can look up fair market prices at Kelly Blue Book (www.KBB.com) or Edmunds (www.Edmunds.com). Paying too much for a car can put you into a bind if you've taken out a loan on the car, because you could end up upside down on the car. This means that you owe more than the car is worth and when you go to sell it, you'll have to pony up extra money to pay off the loan. One way to avoid this is to make sure your down payment is large enough. Only buying cars with good residual value helps too.

Finally, don't buy more car than you can comfortably afford.

**Car Insurance:**

Your car is one of the biggest purchases, after your home, that you will make. Protect that purchase, and yourself, with auto insurance. (If you don't own your car outright, meaning you leased it or have a loan on the car, you will be required to have car insurance and will have to provide proof of insurance to the loan/lease company.) What type and how much insurance will depend on your circumstances and the car you're insuring. Believe it or not, you can have too much insurance.

Let's start with some car insurance terms that you are sure to encounter and will need to understand:

Deductible—The amount you have to pay before insurance goes into effect. If you have a deductible of $500, you pay the first $500 in damages and the insurance company pays for approved costs above that.

Liability Insurance—Insurance that covers damage you cause to another while driving your vehicle. There is Bodily Injury Liability that covers medical bills, loss of income, and pain and suffering and Property Damage Liability that covers the damage to another's vehicle or property (house, fence, mailbox, or whatever else you managed to hit).

Personal Injury Protection—Insurance that covers medical bills for you and the occupants of your vehicle if you are in an accident that you caused.

Comprehensive Insurance—Insurance that covers damage to your vehicle, or any vehicle you are driving, due to a non-accident incident (theft, fire, flood, vandalism, etc.).

Collision Insurance—Insurance that pays for damage to your vehicle due to an accident.

Uninsured and Underinsured Coverage—Insurance that covers your medical bills (and others in your vehicle) if an accident is caused by someone who does not have insurance.

Premium—The amount of money paid to an insurance company in one year in exchange for insurance. The amount can be paid up front or paid in installments—usually monthly.[vi][vii]

Everyone should, at a minimum, purchase liability insurance, which covers damage you cause to someone else. In some states, liability insurance is required by law.

Next you want insurance for you and your vehicle. Get Personal Injury Protection (Medical) to cover the medical bills, lost wages, or (heaven forbid) the funeral for you or anyone in your vehicle.

The decision whether or not to get Comprehensive and Collision insurance will depend on the value of your car. Could you afford to replace your car tomorrow if you had an accident and totaled it? If the answer is 'no', then you should probably get Comprehensive and Collision insurance. If you have a lease or a loan, you'll definitely need to buy Comprehensive and Collision insurance so that if you have an accident, the insurance company will pay to repair or replace the car (after you pay the deductible) and you won't be stuck with a monthly car payment for a car that is in the junkyard.

Gap Insurance (Guaranteed Asset/Auto Protection Insurance) covers the difference between what an insurance company allows for your totaled car and the amount you owe on the car, whether it is a loan or a lease. In other words, if you total the brand new car that you purchased for $20,000 just three months ago and the insurance company only values it at $18,000 because it is now a 'used' car, you'd be liable to the bank for the difference of $2,000. Gap Insurance, which is very reasonable at about $20-30/year, would cover that difference for you. GAP insurance is especially useful on brand new cars or when you haven't put a large down payment on a car. Some leasing companies even require it. If you're interested in purchasing GAP insurance, it is usually less expensive through your insurance company than through the car dealership.

You can choose the amount of your insurance deductible. The higher it is, the cheaper your insurance will be. Make it only as high as you can comfortably afford. Remember, you have to pay the deductible for every incident. Typical deductible amounts are $250, $500 or $1,000.

If you are involved in an accident with another vehicle, always call the police. The police will write an accident report that will include all the information that your insurance company will require in order to pay a claim.

**Car Maintenance:**

Change your oil! If I only had one piece of car maintenance advice, that would be it. Your car will blow up if you don't do this simple chore. (Okay, maybe it won't blow up but it could ruin something that might be very expensive to fix.) Think of it this way: you need food to keep going; your car needs oil to keep going. You can take it to a dealership or to any service station that offers an oil change. (You could change it yourself, however, you would need to dispose of the old oil properly and that can be more trouble and cost than it's worth.) Check your owner's manual to find out how many miles you can drive between oil changes and adhere to it strictly. The manual will also tell you what type of oil to use—synthetic or regular. Most places after they change your oil will put a sticker in the left corner of your windshield telling you when you will be due for another one (if they don't offer it, request it). Don't ignore that sticker.

Oil-change time is a good time to check a few other things like the other fluids in the car (windshield washer, transmission, brake, etc.). Check the treads on your tires. If your tires get too worn down or have a bald or smooth spot, they are prone to sliding or going flat. Also check your windshield wipers. If they are leaving streaks, replace them. Not only is it annoying to try and see through streaks, it can also be dangerous if your visibility is restricted.

Wash your car regularly. Grit and grime will, over time, ruin the paint on a car and cause it to rust. Keeping it cleaned and waxed protects the paint. How often will depend on where you live and whether or not your car is parked in a garage or out in the elements. As a very general recommendation, wash your car every two weeks and wax it twice a year.

If you have leather seats, use a good conditioner on them once a year. It will keep the leather clean and supple and stop it from cracking.

Fix all other issues in a timely manner. If you have a window that won't go up and down or a door handle that is broken, you'll soon start to think of your car as a piece of junk and treat it accordingly. The value of your car as a trade-in will decline drastically.

Here are a few sounds to pay attention to and that signal service is needed. If your brakes start grinding, you need new brake pads. Brakes are an area where unscrupulous mechanics can overcharge you. Front brake jobs shouldn't exceed $300.

From personal experience I can also tell you that if your engine starts making a loud knocking sound, STOP immediately. Do not drive to the nearest exit even if it is only a mile or two away or you will be selling your car to the junk man and renting a car to make it the rest of the way home. Trust me on this one. (Remember, Melissa?)

Lastly, keep all of your service records. If and when you sell the car, you will be able to show a potential buyer that you have been diligent in its upkeep.

**Road Service:**

I highly recommend purchasing a road service plan such as AAA for those pesky road emergencies that come up: flat tire, no gas, keys locked in the car, knocking sound in engine, etc. One call for any of the above services can make AAA's yearly fee worthwhile. (Plus you can use it for discounts at hotels and other businesses.) Like insurance, it buys you peace of mind. Some cars come with road service and it makes sense to utilize that free perk rather than pay extra for AAA.

## Registration and Emission Testing:

You'll have to register your car with your state of residence when you buy it and every year afterward for as long as you own it. Every state is different as far as how much it costs and whether they require emissions testing or not. You can go to your state's DMV (Department of Motor Vehicles) website or you'll find out the answers to those questions when you get your license plate renewal in the mail. You may be able to renew online, but if not, you'll have to go to the DMV near you and wait in line. If you have AAA, you can call to see if an office near you handles registration renewals. Many times the wait times at AAA are much shorter than they are at the DMV. Once you've paid the renewal fee, the DMV will mail you a small sticker and instruct you to adhere it to the corner of your license plate. Do this in a timely manner and it'll give the police one less reason to pull you over for a traffic stop.

## Emergency Supplies:

Your vehicle should come with a spare tire and jack. Do yourself a favor and invest in a flashlight for your car. Jumper cables can come in handy, but aren't a must, especially if you've invested in a road service such as AAA.

If you live in a cold climate, make sure you prepare your car for winter. When you take your car in for an oil change, make sure your antifreeze is good for minus 20-30 degrees Fahrenheit. Fill your windshield wiper fluid and put the rest in the trunk for refilling in slushy weather. All-season tires are fine for some climates, but if you live in an area that gets a lot of snow, you can't beat snow tires for safety. You only need two snow tires--on the front for front-wheel-drive cars or on the rear for rear-wheel-drive cars. Snow tires on my Toyota Corolla was the difference between getting up my driveway or not in a typical Wisconsin winter. Keep a scraper or snowbrush in your car all winter. And it's a good idea to also have a blanket, boots, gloves, and a winter hat in case your car gets stuck and you have to either dig yourself out or walk for help.

If you live in an area prone to earthquakes, you may want to keep a Go-Bag in your car. A Go-Bag should contain a pair of jeans, sneakers, and a jacket along with some emergency water and food (energy bars?). I could go all Prepper on you and talk about emergency radios, solar chargers, water purifiers, and self defense, but that's for another time and another how-to book.

**Driving Safety Tips:**

*Don't drink and drive.* Duh. We all know the consequences of getting a DUI. Not only will it cost you the price of the ticket but possibly your license too. How are you going to get to your job every day to pay for that ticket if you can't drive your car? Your car insurance may take a hit too. Something you may not have considered is the cost to your conscience.

How would you feel if you caused an accident that harmed someone when you had alcohol in your system? Even if it was a true accident, you'd always wonder if your reflexes would have been a tad quicker if you'd been sober. Lastly, an accident that causes injury or death when you've had alcohol in your system is a criminal offense. Being sorry won't save you from paying your debt to society in prison—you made the choice to drink and drive so you are responsible.

*Don't text while driving.* If you thought drinking and driving was bad, studies have shown that texting and driving is six times more dangerous. Texting impairs you visually by causing you to take your eyes off of the road, manually by taking your hands off of the wheel, and cognitively by taking your mind off of your driving. According to the National Highway Traffic Safety Administration (NHTSA), "sending or receiving a text takes a driver's eye from the road for an average of 4.6 seconds, the equivalent—when traveling at 55 mph—of driving the length of an entire football field while blindfolded." [From the Blueprint for Ending Distracted Driving. DOT HS 811 629.][viii]

*Wear your seatbelt.* Not only is it a law in most states, but seat belts are the single most effective way to protect yourself in a crash. Most importantly, seatbelts keep you inside the protective cage of the car. Your chance of being killed increases four-fold if you are thrown from the car.[ix]

*Watch your speed, especially in parking lots and school zones.* Parking lots are breeding grounds for fender benders due to the fact that cars that are backing out of parking spots tend to have very poor visibility. If you are driving through a parking lot and you see a car with its back-up lights lit, don't drive around them shaking your fist at them because you have the right of way. Stop and let them back out safely and hope that you'll receive the same treatment the next time you find your visibility impaired from being parked between two huge SUVs.

*Use the left lane for passing only.* Okay, I threw this one in simply because it's a driving pet peeve of mine. I get so frustrated when drivers sit in the left lane blocking traffic completely oblivious to the line of cars piling up behind them. Drive in the middle or right lanes and save the left lane for passing. There, I feel better.

*"I'm a great believer in luck and I find the harder I work,*

*the more I have of it."*


*- Thomas Jefferson*


# 5 FINDING A JOB

**Where to Look:**

The Internet has changed job hunting forever by creating numerous websites for connecting employers with employees. These sites are constantly changing so do not consider this job hunter's list comprehensive: Craigslist, Monster.com, FindTheRightJob.com, Indeed.com. Know that different industries have job sites dedicated solely to their field. If you have a specific company you're interested in working at, go directly to their site for their current job openings.

## What to Wear:

The type of job you are applying for will determine what to wear to the interview; when in doubt, lean toward the dressier side of what you think is appropriate. For example, if you are applying for any kind of office job, dress professionally (for women, this means a dress, skirt or dress pants and nice top; for guys this means dress pants and a long-sleeved shirt at the least and possibly a coat and tie). Never wear jeans, t-shirts, or tennis shoes to an office interview. Jeans may be acceptable for some job interviews, but pair them with a neat, pressed, unstained and collared shirt. Show your respect for the job and the interviewer by being showered and combed and having a neat appearance. No hats or t-shirts, especially ones with questionable or objectionable graphics. Hide any tattoos or piercings that may be considered inappropriate for the job you're applying for.

## What to Bring:

*Resume.* If you have a resume, obviously you should bring it with you to every job interview. Ideally you should update your resume every time you leave a job while the information is fresh in your mind (dates, contacts, duties, etc.) and so that your resume is always up to date. A complete, professional resume demonstrates attention to detail. A stand-out resume demonstrates creativity.

*List of questions.* Be prepared with your own intelligent questions to ask your interviewer. Remember that you are interviewing the company at the same time that they are interviewing you. (Please do not let your first questions be "how much will I make?" and "how much vacation do I get?") Here are some examples that might be appropriate:

1. What does the head of the department look for in personal characteristics?

2. What are the expectations of performance in this position? How is performance measured?

3. What are the opportunities for advancement?

4. What happened to the previous person in the position? (You particularly want to know if they were promoted, and if so, to what position. If they tell you they were let go or quit, ask why.)

5. What is the importance of the other team members? What are their roles? How do they work together?

## Interview Tips:

1. Be prepared. Research the company ahead of the interview. If they've been in the news lately, comment on it (unless, of course, it was for a scandal or some other negative reason—yikes).

2. Show controlled enthusiasm but don't look needy. Want is good; need is bad.

3. Be honest. Admitting a fault, mistake or regret is always better than being caught in a lie. Don't be evasive.

4. Be yourself. Show them your personality. They want to know how you'll fit in with their other employees.

5. Don't share specific salary expectations; do relate to fair compensation for the responsibilities of the job. Answer directly if asked about your current salary; however, relate it to *why* you are looking for a new job. Example: your salary has not kept up with the added responsibilities you have been given.

6. Think about where you want to be in five or ten years. What kind of position and what responsibilities would you like to have? Be realistic but be aggressive.

## Before, During and After the Interview:

Whether you've made an appointment or you just walked in off the street, first impressions are important. Always be polite, be on time, look professional/presentable, speak clearly, make eye contact, stand up straight and be confident (even if you don't feel it). Make sure you thank the interviewer for their time and consideration. Send a follow-up email or note to thank them again for their time. By following up, you are showing that you are interested in the job and you are giving them one more reason to remember your name.

## Be Careful with Social Media:

Be aware that more and more employers are using social media (Facebook, Instagram, and Twitter) to check up on potential and current employees. Keep your posts positive and respectful. Never use profanity or post embarrassing or lewd photographs of yourself. And remember that if you call in sick at work, *do not* post pictures of yourself at the baseball game or beach.

*"What does friends with benefits even mean? Does he provide her with health insurance?"*


*- Sheldon Cooper, character from the TV show The Big Bang Theory*


# 6 MEDICAL ISSUES


**Health Insurance:**

As of 2014 and the passing of the ACA (Affordable Care Act), every American is required to have health insurance. If your employer offers you health insurance, be grateful and say "thank you" and sign up. If your employer does not provide it, you may go online to HealthCare.gov and check out your options. Depending on your income, you may qualify for subsidies to help you pay your premium. This is a constantly changing situation, so that's all I'll say about that for now.


Health insurance does not mean free health care. Health insurance helps to keep your medical expenses manageable. Most of the time, health insurance will just pay a portion of your doctor visit, prescription, procedure or hospital costs. How large of a portion will depend on the type of plan you have (HSA, HMO, PPO) and the deductibles and co-pays associated with your plan. Each plan is different, so know and understand your insurance policy.

An *HSA (Health Savings Account)* is a medical savings account paired with a high-deductible health insurance plan. You (and sometimes your employer) contribute pre-tax money into a savings account set up exclusively for medical expenses. You then use that account to pay for all approved medical expenses up until the insurance deductible is met at which point your insurance kicks in. HSAs are favorites among those who are generally healthy and have relatively fewer medical expenses. Unused funds accumulate, tax free, and remain the property of the account holder (even if their employer has contributed to it) until retirement age at which point the funds can be used for any purpose. Like an IRA, funds are taxed when money is withdrawn from the account (unless used for approved medical expenses) and a 20% penalty is assessed if withdrawn before the age of 65. Check current laws for maximum allowable yearly contributions.

An *HMO (Health Maintenance Organization)* means you receive all of your health care from a specific network of doctors and hospitals. You must choose a primary care physician who serves as the starting point for all of your medical care. If you need to see a specialist, your primary care physician must refer you to one in order for the service to be covered. Your health insurance will only cover doctors in that specific network. HMOs tend to be less expensive than PPOs and may offer more preventative care than other plans but they may be more restrictive as to the doctors and hospitals that are covered.

A *PPO (Preferred Provider Organization)*, like an HMO, also has a network of contracted health care providers (doctors and hospitals) but they don't require you to use them. You may go to any doctor or hospital that you choose, however, you will pay more out of pocket if you use a provider that is outside of the preferred network. Your plan will tell you exactly what those rates/percentages are. PPOs are generally slightly more expensive than HMOs but offer more choice in providers.

A *copay is a fee charged at the time of service* and usually applies to doctor visits or prescriptions. For example, a doctor visit may require a $50 copay which you pay at the appointment but then the rest of the visit is covered by insurance. Copays are the insurance company's way of keeping costs down. If you have to pay *something* for a service, hopefully you won't abuse the availability of the service. Many times the copay will go up for more specialized services (i.e. $10 copay for a generic drug, $20 for a name-brand drug, and $60 for a proprietary drug).

The *deductible is the amount you must pay out of pocket before your insurance company pays*. For example, a health insurance policy might have a $1,500, $2,500 or $5,000 deductible which means if you have to go to the hospital for an accident or illness, you are responsible for the deductible amount and your insurance will start paying after the deductible has been met. But it doesn't necessarily mean that your insurance will pay for everything after that. Some policies have limits up to a certain dollar amount (lifetime maximums) or some pay for only a percentage of the total bill such as 80% (coinsurance) after the deductible is met.

If your plan is through your employer, you may not have a choice of what type of plan is offered or the related deductibles. If you do have a choice, either through your employer or because you are self-insured, pick the plan that best fits your needs but that is still affordable. It will be a compromise. Typically, the lower the deductibles and copays associated with a health plan, the higher the monthly health insurance premiums. Don't be afraid to ask questions if you don't understand your plan or your plan options.

## Where to Go for Medical Care:

Where to go for medical care will depend on the medical situation. Ideally you will have a primary care physician that you see regularly, maybe for yearly check-ups, who has your whole health history on file and who you can call when a health issue crops up. If not, don't worry—you're not alone. Young people especially have fewer health issues and therefore may have never established a relationship with a doctor. If you don't have a regular doctor and you would like some care/a diagnosis/medicine, you can simply visit a clinic or an urgent care center near you. Some large drug store chains have walk-in clinics in them (CVS, Walgreens). Avoid hospital emergency rooms unless your situation is truly an emergency. Emergency rooms are chaotic places and they will see patients not in the order of arrival but according to the severity of the emergency. If you go there for an ear infection, for example, you will not be high on their list and you could wait all day to see a doctor.

In a perfect world, you will have done your homework before you got sick or hurt and located the doctors and/or clinics near you that are covered by your insurance. That way, when you need a throat culture to see if you have strep throat or an x-ray because your arm is bent at an odd angle, you don't have to first spend time doing research at your computer to locate a preferred provider in your area.

Some health insurance plans now offer a 'call-a-nurse' service for those times when you're not sure if you need to see a doctor. You describe your symptoms to the nurse and she tells you whether you can stay home and treat yourself with rest and lots of fluids or that you should get your butt over to the doctor's office pronto. She may save you a trip to the doctor and the resulting copay or fee (and also give you some peace of mind), so keep that number in your phone at all times.

I'd like to add one more thing in the spirit of keeping health care costs down in this country. If each of us would shop for health care like we shop for everything else in our lives, meaning we shop for value, we could all do our part to lower health-related costs. When you see a doctor or pick up a prescription at a pharmacy, ask what the price of the product or service is. Educate yourself about what things cost—not your portion of the bill or the copay, but the actual price as if you didn't have insurance. I think you'd be surprised not only by the charges themselves, but by the difference in what providers charge for the exact same products or services. Prescriptions can vary by 100% or more depending on where you buy them. Clinics that specialize in x-rays or scans can offer huge savings over the same services at a hospital. Those price differences aren't something most people are aware of because all they pay is their copay, and that's the same no matter where they go. But insurance companies care and they factor the higher costs into their renewal rates.

I think you get the idea. Be a conscientious buyer of health care services. Buy generics when they are available. Don't go to the emergency room for routine care. Get your blood work done at a lab (Quest, LabCorp) and your x-rays at a clinic rather than at a hospital (I'm referring to scheduled tests, not emergency procedures, of course). It may not save you any money today, but it could help to keep your insurance rates down in the future.

**Dental Care:**

I'm sure I don't have to tell you to brush your teeth—those are instructions for a 5-year old and you probably do it without complaint at least twice a day.

A better question is whether or not you floss every day. My guess is, probably not. But you should. Flossing is a tougher sell because the benefits are more long-term—healthy gums. What if I told you that an immediate benefit of flossing is better breath? It's true. It gets rid of the bacteria that collects between your teeth that gives you bad breath. You should brush your tongue too—it's another bacteria breeding ground.

For optimal oral hygiene, you should have your teeth cleaned twice a year. The better you are about flossing and brushing, the less tartar buildup there will be and, therefore, the less painful your cleanings will be. Once a year the dentist will take x-rays to check for cavities or other issues. At the time of this writing, there is a debate about whether annual exposure to the radiation from x-rays is wise and necessary. Some believe that the discomfort of a cavity or other dental issue will dictate when you need an x-ray. Others believe x-rays help to find problems in their early stages (infections, tumors, diseases) and are therefore still an important annual tool. Since it's still a free country, you can decide for yourself how often to get dental x-rays.

**Dental Insurance:**

Should you or shouldn't you purchase dental insurance? If your employer offers it and it's free—yippee, then of course you should take it. (Who turns down free stuff?) If it requires a small contribution on your part, you should still consider it.

Having dental insurance makes it painless (at least on your wallet) to have those bi-annual cleanings. However, if you have to pay the full cost of dental insurance, it's a gamble as to whether it will be worth it or not. The cost of two cleanings and one set of x-rays is usually cheaper than the dental insurance premiums you'd pay over the year. You'd realize the benefit of insurance if you had a cavity, needed a root canal or had some other dental emergency. Those are the procedures that can do some serious damage to your bank account.

## Health and Wellness:

Eat right. Exercise. Get enough sleep. Drink plenty of water. Take your vitamins. Don't smoke. Get your vaccinations. Spend time outside. Meditate. You know what to do.

## Safe Sex:

Do we even have to get into this? You all know about safe sex, right?

Shoot. Okay, just in case, I'll give you the basics. First and foremost, USE A CONDOM! That's safe sex in a nutshell (besides the most effective birth control of all—abstinence). I'm assuming here that you know that just using birth control isn't enough to prevent AIDS or an STD (sexually transmitted disease) or an STI (sexually transmitted infection)—it just prevents pregnancy. You can get AIDS or an STD even if you are on the pill, have an IUD (intra-uterine device), or use the morning-after pill because infections are passed through contact and/or fluids. So protect yourself by using a condom every time. You should avoid sex altogether with anyone who is experiencing any type of breakout—a rash, genital sores or warts. And never use an oil-based lubricant (like Vaseline) with a condom—it breaks down the latex in the condom and could cause the condom to fail.

The only time you should have sex without a condom is if you and your partner are monogamous (you only have sex with each other) and you've waited six months since you've both been tested and cleared. Don't be naïve and don't rely on your partner's word—insist they get tested. Be aware that there are no good tests for herpes—it can lay dormant and you might not even know you have it until you have a breakout.

For HIV and STD testing, consult your doctor, visit a clinic, or find a Planned Parenthood near you. (Planned Parenthood can also provide free contraceptives.) If you didn't get the HPV vaccine (human papillomavirus—the most common sexually-transmitted virus in the US) when you were 11 or 12, it is available for both guys and girls up to the age of 26. It is most effective before you become sexually active (too late?). You should also make sure you have received a vaccination for hepatitis B. Again, ask your doctor or visit a clinic or Planned Parenthood for access to both of those.[x][xi]

*"Note to self: when I eat like crap I feel like crap."*

*- Unknown*

# 7 FOOD

Grocery shopping can be an eye opener for the recently emancipated. You will discover a new appreciation for the sheer amount of food your parents routinely kept in their refrigerators and pantries and you'll remember with nostalgia all of the times you whined, "there's nothing to eat in this house!" Even though grocery shopping can be expensive, eating out is probably the biggest budget buster there is. When going out, remember it is more than just the cost of the menu item you order. It is also the drinks (which can add up to more than the food portion of your bill very quickly), tip, tax, and parking or transportation fees.

**Eating Healthy:**

Did you know that 70-80% of your immune system is in your digestive tract? That means having a healthy diet decreases your chance of getting sick. A healthy diet is a balanced diet eaten in moderation. We in America are used to super-sizing and huge portions. One theory floating around is that we are constantly hungry because we consume so many empty calories from processed foods and junk foods. If we would eat foods that are high in nutritional value, we'd feel sated sooner. An easy way to do that is to eat more whole foods (foods that have ONE ingredient, i.e. eggs have eggs in them, an apple is made up of . . . . yep, an apple). I've found that shopping on the outer edges of the grocery store rather than in the aisles helps. It's on the outer edges that you find produce, dairy, and meats. The aisles contain boxed and bagged items full of preservatives. Eat the fresh stuff. Better yet, eat local fresh stuff—shop at farmers' markets or produce stands. Try to switch away from the 'whites' (sugar, rice, bread, and pasta) to raw sugar and whole grains. Are you a soda drinker? Try to wean yourself off of it; it's bad stuff. Switch to water; it's good for you and it's cheap. In fact, eating healthy will save you money all kinds of ways: you'll have fewer expensive health issues, fewer sick days at work, and no expensive weight loss programs!

**Cooking:**

Cooking easy meals doesn't have to mean cracking open a box of Mac and Cheese. If cooking is completely foreign to you, start small. Start with an easy recipe that just involves boiling water—like pasta for instance. Boil some water, add the pasta (preferably whole wheat pasta), cook for 10 minutes or so, and drain in a colander. Now, in the same pan you boiled the pasta, add some simple toppings such as a diced tomato, olive oil, salt and pepper and toss along with the drained pasta. Sometimes the classiest meals are also the simplest. Give it a fancy touch by serving it in an over-sized pasta bowl. Maybe throw some fresh parsley or basil on top for color and serve it with sparkling water or wine and a salad. Voila. You'd impress any date with that meal.

You can broaden your cooking skills by baking simple meals in the oven. Buy a chicken breast (hormone and antibiotic free, preferably), rub it in olive oil, salt, and pepper, put it in a glass baking dish and bake it at 350 degrees for 30-40 minutes. You've just made baked chicken. If you'd like, cube a few potatoes or yams and throw them in the dish with the chicken. Maybe add some broccoli. You've got a complete meal made in one dish using all whole foods and ready to eat in under an hour—all with minimum effort.

By starting small and getting comfortable with a couple of easy meals, you may even develop an interest in cooking and broaden your skills. It's easy to learn more. Find recipes online—many come with instructional videos. As a 20-year-old new wife and mother, my cooking savior was my Betty Crocker Cookbook. Betty didn't assume that I knew how to do anything or that I knew what all the cooking terms meant—she explained everything. Some people laughed at me because I didn't know how to boil an egg. Not Betty—she explained it step by step and even gave me more than one method to do it.

You have to start somewhere; people aren't born knowing how to chop garlic or how to cut up a pineapple. Experiment. Don't be afraid to try new things. Check out companies like Blue Apron to get healthy recipes and fresh ingredients shipped directly to you. Make it fun by cooking with a friend or a date. Be willing to have a flop and laugh about it afterward.

## Kitchen Supplies:

To get your kitchen started, start with some simple supplies. At a minimum, you'll want a 9-quart-or-so kettle, a 10-inch-or-so frying pan and a 9 x 13 pan for baking. Basic utensils to have on hand include a wooden spoon, a whisk, a spatula, a can opener and a scraper. If there were an area to splurge and pay a little more, it would be for knives. Better to have just a few quality knives than a whole butcher block full of cheap knives. Start with a sharp paring knife and an all-purpose Santoku knife. Buy a knife sharpener and learn how to use it; a sharp knife is less dangerous than a dull knife. And buy a cutting board. You can build your kitchen supplies from there as your interest and experience broadens.

*"You're off to great places!*

*Today is your day!*

*Your mountain is waiting,*

*So . . . get on your way!"*

-    Dr. Seuss

# 8 TRAVEL

I hope you get a chance to travel. Traveling offers you experiences that broaden your thinking and memories that stay with you forever.

When I travel, especially when leaving the U.S., I like to live like the locals. I eat the local food, stay in small inns where I can meet the owners or innkeepers, and visit the local pubs or small coffee shops. These are the places to get the real flavor of the area. I figure that if I want to eat American food and talk to Americans, why not just stay home? So my advice to you when you travel is to be adventurous. Talk to the locals, attempt to speak a new language, eat the local food at the places that the locals prefer. You'd be amazed at how much can be communicated through sign language, a smile, and the words 'please' and 'thank you'. And remember that when you travel out of the U.S., you represent your country—so be a good ambassador of the United States.

**Air Travel:**

This section is for budget travelers. If money is no object, then simply call your travel agent and ask them to book you a first-class seat to whichever exotic location you're heading to and put on those cute jammies they give you so you can sleep comfortably in your fully-reclined seat with your feather pillow. (Yes, they really do that in first-class overseas flights—you even get eye masks to block out the light! If I sound jealous it's because I am. It is my goal to someday be able to afford a first-class overseas ticket.)

For the rest of us, it pays to know how to work the system. When I'm looking for flights, I like to go to a travel site that compares airlines so that I can find not only the best prices but also the most convenient times and the least number of layovers. I use Kayak.com because they not only search airlines but also other discount travel sites, and once you find a flight you like, they connect you directly with that airline or discount site. (I prefer to book directly through the airline rather than a travel site because I find that the information is more accurate, seating is more reliable, and schedule changes are conveyed to me more efficiently.) There are many travel sites out there. Find the one that suits you.

When comparing prices, remember to factor in fees. Some (most) airlines tack on extra charges for baggage, seating (not only exit row but sometimes even for a window or an aisle), and change fees (if you have to change or cancel your flight, you can be charged fees of $150 or more per flight PLUS the difference in the cost of the fare). For that reason, I'm a big fan of Southwest Airlines. Even for their lowest rates, their Wanna Get Away rates, they allow each passenger two free checked bags and they have no change fees.

Save money on airline tickets by booking early (especially for holiday travel) and traveling mid week. Friday, Sunday and Monday travel are usually the busiest days to fly, so avoid those when you can.

You can earn air miles whenever you fly by registering for the frequent flyer program of each airline. If you have a favorite airline, you may even want to apply for their credit card. Most offer a mile for every dollar spent on the card so it's a great way to rack up air miles quickly.

## Car Rentals:

The ability of someone under the age of 26 to rent a car depends on both the state they are renting in and the rental car company. Do a search for your destination state and your age to get the latest information. I remember a time when I wanted my son, who was 18 at the time, to be able to drive my rental car for just one of the four days we would be in New York state. We rented a car at La Guardia and I paid an extra $400 for him to be able to drive the car that one day only to find out that had we rented our car at the airport in Newark, NJ, it would have cost us a fraction of the price.

It's practically a necessity to have a credit card before you can rent a car. Many credit cards offer rental car insurance. If you know that the credit card you are using to rent a car offers rental insurance, DO NOT buy the insurance offered by the rental car company. Accepting and paying for liability insurance when you rent a car nullifies the insurance that your credit card company offers.

Another option for insuring a rental car is through your regular car insurance. Some policies cover damage to rental cars and some offer it as an inexpensive rider on your policy.

It's worth a phone call to both your auto insurance company and your credit card company to find out if and what they cover regarding rental cars.

If you are renting a car in a foreign country, definitely make those phone calls to your credit card company or insurance company to inquire specifically about what they cover in the country you are visiting. We went to Europe a few years ago and planned to travel through several countries. We were surprised to find out that Ireland was one of the countries where our credit card did not offer rental car insurance. Let me clarify. We were surprised until we pulled out of the rental lot. Then we knew exactly why the credit card companies don't insure rental cars in Ireland. The roads in Ireland are very narrow with hedgerows lining both sides of the road. When a car (or way worse, a bus or truck) is heading toward you on Ireland's very narrow roads, the tendency is to lean towards the hedgerow side of the road to avoid a head-on collision. Unfortunately, hedgerows are notorious for scratching the paint on cars that rub up against them. Our car, which had been brand new and unscathed when we drove it out of the Hertz rental lot, was returned by us a week later with a solid line of scratches the entire length of the car. Plus, our right side-view mirror was gone, snapped off by a truck when we didn't lean sufficiently close enough to the hedgerow. When we returned our rental car to the Hertz lot, they said that it had been 'Americanized'. Apparently, we were not the only ones to have a problem with the skinny roads of Ireland and driving on the left-hand side of the road.

One more useful tidbit about renting cars. The best rates are the weekend or weekly rates. Renting for 4-5 days in the middle of the week usually costs as much as an entire week, so plan your trip accordingly. Also, you can pick up the car in one location and return it somewhere else; however, you will pay a drop-off fee to do that. To get the best rental car rates, rent for a weekend (which can include four days: Thurs-Sun or Fri-Monday) or a week and return the car to the same place that you picked it up.

## Hotels:

Are you booking a hotel without a reservation? Maybe you are on a long driving trip and just need a place to crash so that you can get up in the morning and hit the road again. There are several apps out there that can help find hotels nearby that have a vacancy: Hotel Tonight, Hotels.com, Expedia, Last Minute Travel Deals, Hotel Now, Travelocity, JetSetter, and Orbitz, just to name a few. Or, you can do it the old-fashioned way and simply stop at a chain that you recognize close to the freeway. You take a chance that the hotel may be full, but if it isn't, same-day bookings can yield the best prices (unlike with airfares). My favorite way of getting the lowest price for a room is by asking about their rates and then asking the simple question "is that the best you can do?" This one question cuts through all of the red tape and simply asks for the lowest rate that the hotel clerk is allowed to give based on their occupancy. I was given this hint by a friend who managed a large hotel chain. He said that most hotels give their clerks a price that they are allowed to offer rather than have a potential customer walk out the door. It doesn't work every time, but it works often enough that it is worth asking the question.

Are you planning a trip and want to reserve a room ahead of time? Then you should do your homework and use a website such as hotels.com or kayak.com where they search for the lowest price for you. You can see pictures of the lobby and the rooms (I always look for hotels that use duvets rather than bedspreads after viewing a disturbing expose in which a black light was aimed at hotel bedspreads and showed an absurd number of body fluid stains on all of them—disgusting, but I digress) and read a couple of reviews. Reviews might highlight an extra charge for parking or a resort fee or an undesirable attribute such as road noise or a musty smell.

No matter what the booking circumstances, don't forget to ask if they offer a AAA discount (that is, of course, if you have AAA). It could save you up to 10%.

## Traveling Abroad (passports, visas, currency, cell phones, packing):

*Passports:* A passport is required almost every time you leave the United States. If you don't already have one, you should get one now. Getting one when you're not in a rush will save you money and stress later.

If this is your first passport, you must apply in person (whereas renewals can usually be done by mail). Download Form DS-11 at http://www.state.gov/documents/organization/212239.pdf

or pick one up at any post office, fill it out (but **don't sign it—** you must sign it in person when you apply), assemble the documents required (a list of acceptable documents can be found on the back of Form DS-11 or at http://travel.state.gov/content/passports/english/passports/ new.html ) and take it to a qualifying post office, DMV, clerk of courts office, or library. You can find the places nearest you that will accept your application here: http://iafdb.travel.state.gov.

There is such a thing as a Passport Office in certain major cities around the country, but you should only take it there if you're traveling in less than two weeks. Know that you will need an appointment and there will be additional fees when you go through a Passport Office.

You will need a passport photo. You can take it yourself using these guidelines (https://www.epassportphoto.com) or have one taken for a nominal fee either at the post office, local AAA office, or at most photo processing centers (CVS, Walgreens, Walmart, Sam's, Costco, Fed Ex or UPS store, etc.). At the time of this printing, passports cost $135 for a new passport (16 or older), $105 for a minor, and $110 for a renewal. The typical processing time is 4-6 weeks. If you need it sooner, expediting fees apply.

*Visas:* You may be required to get a travel visa to visit a foreign country. Go to http://travel.state.gov/content/passports/english/country.ht ml and plug in the country (or countries) that you will be visiting. There you will be advised as to whether or not you need a visa to enter that country. It will also list any required or suggested vaccinations and relay any travel advisories or warnings.

*Currency/credit or debit cards when traveling:* How are you planning on paying for things when you are traveling outside the US? How will you pay for a taxi or a snack at the airport?

Know that exchanging currency always involves a fee but you can minimize those fees by exchanging your money in the best places. The highest fees are charged at the exchange booths at or near the airport where people who haven't planned ahead are desperate for the local currency.

My preferred money strategy when I travel abroad involves leaving the U.S. with a small amount of my destination's currency ($100-$300) that I got at my bank or local AAA office. After that, I use my credit card for larger purchases such as hotels or car rentals and my debit card at an ATM to replenish my local currency as needed. Typically, withdrawing cash using your debit card will cost less than a money exchanger. (If you plan on using your credit card to get cash, make sure you know the PIN associated with that card before you leave the U.S.)

Which credit card should you use? Credit cards are not created equally when it comes to international travel. The best cards for travel are Visa or MasterCard because they are accepted virtually everywhere. American Express is gaining acceptance in more places while Discover is not widely accepted outside the U.S. Be aware that most credit cards will charge a currency transaction fee every time you use your card (usually in the range of 2-3%).

Call your credit card company before you leave the country to avoid the hassle of their fraud department putting your credit card on hold when they see a charge from a foreign country. It's also a good idea to take at least two credit cards with you for the same reason. If you have trouble with one card, you'll have a backup to use until the misunderstanding has been cleared up.

*Cell phones:* If you'd like to have access to a phone when traveling internationally, you have several options. You can take your own phone, you can rent an international travel phone, or you can buy a disposable phone when you get to your destination. Which option you choose depends on your situation. Do you want people to reach you at your own number or would you like to have access to the phonebook on your phone? Will you use your phone for emergencies only or will you be using it regularly? How long will you be traveling?

Using a U.S.-based phone in another country means you will be charged international fees. So, to avoid coming home to a cell phone bill in the thousands of dollars (you wouldn't be the first) check with your cell phone company before you leave to come up with the best strategy for you to minimize costs. Most phone companies offer international plans, either temporary or permanent, that charge by the minute and/or the country. Some offer international texting plans too. Consider adding the Skype app to your phone so that you can make calls for free when connected to the internet. Most importantly, if you have a smart phone, make sure you turn off data roaming under 'Settings' to avoid incurring charges even when you're not talking on your phone.

Note: If you decide to buy a local phone to use during your stay, get it from a reputable store—do not purchase one off the street to get a good deal. Chances are, the person selling it is looking for a naïve foreigner to pull a scam on. Also know that cell phones, like expensive jewelry, can attract thieves. Be discreet when using your phone and keep it out of sight in a safe place when it is not in use.

*Packing:* I don't mean to brag, but I'm somewhat of a packing expert. My claim to fame is that I went to Europe for a month with only one piece of luggage that fit in the overhead compartment.

My secret is layering. And a minimal number of shoes. And the ability to do laundry along the way. My motivation is my husband's policy of 'if you pack it, you carry it.'

I recommend one suitcase with wheels that, size-wise, pushes the boundaries of what is considered a carry-on bag. You will remember my advice and appreciate it when you check in to that five-story hotel with no elevator or when you're climbing the three flights of stairs leading out of the train station in Paris.

The weather can make packing light tricky. Layering solves that problem by allowing you to start with a short-sleeved shirt and add a long-sleeved shirt and/or a jacket if needed (or vice versa—removing items as the day warms up). Keep your outfits simple and classic and interchangeable. Remember, if you don't love it and wear it often at home, you won't wear it on vacation either. Forget the American custom of wearing fresh clothes every day. For a jacket, I recommend a medium-weight, all-purpose jacket (weatherproof too, if possible) that can be dressed up for evenings or dressed down for daytime activities. Shoes are all about comfort. Take two pairs—one for daytime and lots of walking, the other a little nicer for evenings but also good for walking. Take only one belt that matches both shoes and, for women, one purse that matches every outfit and has at least one zippered compartment for valuables such as your passport and credit cards.

*"Manners are a sensitive awareness of the feelings of others. If you have that awareness, you have good manners, no matter which fork you use."*

- *Emily Post*

# 9 PERSONAL

**Manners:**

Good manners have almost become passé today. As a society we have become more casual and we have let some manners fall away because they represent a more formal time. I believe that there are some basic manners that should never go away because they show a respect for and an awareness of your fellow human being.

Let's start with the basics—greetings. It's polite to acknowledge someone when they walk in the room or, if you're the one entering the room, to acknowledge everyone in it (I am, of course, referring to a home setting, not a public place). A grunt does not count. Take a moment to look each person in the eye and say hello (or 'hi' or 'greetings' or 'sup'— or whatever is cool these days). When meeting someone face-to-face, it is appropriate to offer to shake their hand. This custom goes way back and served as a gesture of peace by demonstrating that the hand didn't hold a weapon. A handshake should have the proper firmness. Too firm and it signals aggression or over compensation; too light and it shows a lack of confidence. Give a Goldilocks handshake—just the right pressure to convey that you are confident and friendly. One exception to shaking hands, however, is if you have a cold. Then you should avoid passing on your germs and decline the handshake. The receiver of the handshake will thank you for it.

Ask for things, don't demand them. For example, "may I please have the remote?" will get the desired response more often than "gimme the damn remote" which will more than likely get you a lump on the head.

Say "excuse me." I'm sure your first thought went to bodily functions. That's actually good. But don't forget to excuse yourself when you bump into someone, when you interrupt them, or when you need them to move so you can get around them.

Use "please" and "thank you" a lot. In France, they recommend saying "s'il vous plait" and "merci" in just about every sentence—especially in formal situations or with strangers. (I found the French to be perfectly hospitable people—completely at odds with their international reputation and from what I'd heard from others—whenever I used my pleases and thank yous. I wonder if all that the French people want is for tourists to show some manners and then they will respond in kind).

Don't wear a hat to the dinner table. Or to church or to the theater (especially if it's a big hat and it blocks the view of people behind you—I hate when that happens).

If you're a guy, stand when a girl enters the room. And hold her chair out for her. Girls are suckers for gallantry. If you're confused about the whole women's lib thing, think of it this way: most women I know are all for women's rights when it comes to equal job opportunities and equal pay for equal work, but they still appreciate being treated like a woman when it comes to manners.

Hold the door for people. This goes for all of us, guys and girls. It's simply not nice to let a door slam in someone's face. And this is especially true if the person has their hands full. I remember an incident when I was heading into a store, pushing a large stroller that contained a newborn and a toddler while struggling to keep a diaper bag and a purse from falling off of my shoulder. I had hoped and assumed that the gentleman ahead of me would hold the door for me since all of my hands were already occupied, but I was mistaken. The door slammed into my stroller and he never even looked back to see what the crash was about. Being helpful and polite shows that you care about others and are not just in this world for yourself. Hold a door for someone, extend an arm to an elderly person who is stepping up a curb, let someone go ahead of you. Just be kind to each other. Some day you might be that person who needs the helping hand.

**Phone Etiquette:**

This is a huge topic these days. In the 'old days,' phone etiquette simply meant answering the phone politely ("hello, Suzie speaking") and taking a proper message. Cell phones have expanded not only the availability of phones but also the abuses of them. Try to remember that your phone is a tool, not an obligation. You bought the phone and you pay your phone bill so you get to decide when and how you use your phone. Not all calls and texts need an immediate response. Voicemail was invented so you can take and return calls at your convenience.

If you feel you must take a call in public, excuse yourself to a more private area where your conversation won't compete with the other conversations in the room. If you can't remove yourself (let's say you're in a car or plane where stepping outside could be painful), then keep the call short and speak quietly. We've all heard the multitude of conversations that erupt as soon as a plane lands and phones are allowed. Passengers reach for their phones like a smoker goes for his cigarette.

Make an effort to keep your phone out of site in restaurants or at the dinner table. Turn off your ringer in theaters, church, school or the library. Hang up your phone before going through a check-out line. Don't put your phone on speaker in public—if I didn't want to hear your side of a phone call, then I certainly don't want to suffer through both sides of the call.

Just because we *can* take our phones everywhere and talk on them anywhere doesn't mean we should. My simple advice is to use common sense and have courtesy for those around you. Be present in the life that is occurring right in front of you rather than worrying about what may be going on in your electronic life.

## Tipping:

In America, it is proper to tip your server at a restaurant. The standard tip is 15% (however, my daughter, the waitress, would prefer you leave 20%). Obviously, the quality of service will determine the exact amount. If your server went above and beyond (think 10 soda refills), leave a little extra to show your appreciation. If you used a Groupon to buy one meal and got the other for free, tip on what the whole amount would have been. The Groupon is from the restaurant—the server still has the same amount of work to do and most likely didn't plan on having his/her tips halved because the owner ran a promotion. Know that servers usually receive a lower hourly wage because of the expectation of a tip and restaurants are able to charge you less because of it. So when dining out, include the tip in your budget. If you can't afford to tip your server, maybe you should go out for fast food instead.

There are others in the service industry who make a full wage for what they do but hope for a tip as a sign of appreciation that they've gone above and beyond in their duties. In the case of hairdressers or other beauty technicians, bellboys, maids, bartenders, taxi drivers, and tour guides, to name a few, use your discretion as to when and how much you should tip them.

**Thank Yous:**

I'm a huge fan of sending a thank you note when someone has done something nice for me. Not only is it good manners, but it's a way for the giver to know that their gift has been received and appreciated. How awful it is to mail someone a birthday gift or a wedding card with money in it and to wonder if it ever made it. You don't want to call and ask if they got it because it feels like you're looking for a pat on the back. However, if they didn't receive your gift, they could walk around for the rest of their lives thinking you were a cheapskate because you didn't send them a wedding gift. Technology has made the thank you note a simple thing. If you don't want to take the time to write a note and mail it, you can simply send an email or a text.

**Hostess Gift:**

It is appropriate to bring a gift if you've been invited to someone's house for a meal. It's a way of saying thank you for the effort and expense that the host most probably spent on the preparation. The go-to gift is a bottle of wine (in the $10-20 range). Remember that the bottle is a gift and, whereas the host may very well open it that evening, you shouldn't expect them too. If you don't bring wine, you could bring flowers or any small token of appreciation such as a pound of your favorite coffee, a kitchen gadget, or even something homemade. Think about what you'd appreciate if the roles were reversed.

**Weddings:**

You are entering the wedding age when your friends will start announcing that they are engaged and getting married. How wonderful, how romantic . . . . how expensive. How bad can it be? You are invited to a fun party where there's free food and sometimes even free drinks.

Well, the wedding is only the final event of the process of 'getting married'. You may be invited to an engagement dinner (where a gift is optional), then a bridal shower (guys, you're not in the clear on this, it could be a Couple's Shower) and the expected shower gift, a bachelor or bachelorette party with the requisite gag gifts and alcohol, possibly a rehearsal dinner, and then, finally the big event, the wedding, where you certainly are expected to give a gift. You can only hope that the wedding is nearby so that you don't also have to plan for flights and hotels. You should, however, factor in the cost of the proper apparel for each event. All in all, weddings are becoming quite the social events and therefore, quite the strain on the checkbook.

To combat this assault to your bank account, you may want to get a second job. Just kidding. (Or am I?)

Some expenses are just a fact of life. If you're invited to a wedding, manners dictate that you give the newlyweds a gift. The amount you spend will depend on two things: how close of a friend/relative the bride or groom is and your budget. A wedding gift doesn't have to be fancy. It can be practical or fun or meaningful.

If you're asked to be a bridesmaid or groomsman (wait, I'm being sexist—these days there are also bridesmen and groomswomen), know that there will be additional costs such as throwing showers or bachelor/bachelorette parties and special wedding clothing (dresses, tuxes, shoes, etc.). If you don't feel you are able to handle the costs, you may want to turn down a friend's request to be in their wedding. It's best to be honest up front rather than embarrassed later when you can't live up to your obligations.

**Organization Tips:**

Being organized comes easily to some but is a great mystery to others. For me, organization means everything in its place, an up-to-date calendar, and lots of lists.

*A Place for Everything and Maybe it's the Trash Can:* I already talked about putting things away in the section on Apartments but let me expand on that as it relates to organization. Obviously our home is where we keep our stuff. But probably a more pertinent question is how much stuff do we need? I'm going to generalize here but, we Americans, we like our stuff. Some of us like clothes, some like electronics, some like collectibles . . . there's nothing wrong with that. We all should have hobbies and passions and interests. But sometimes we get into the habit of keeping things that don't really serve us; they are not our passions. Usually it is simply a case of not taking the time to think about it to consciously decide whether it's worth keeping or not.

So, I'm recommending that you try to be more mindful when deciding what to keep and what to toss. When you buy a new pair of tennis shoes, throw out the old ones. Otherwise you know you are just going to toss them into the back of the closet where you'll find them, covered in dust, during your next move.

When the mail comes, don't just let it pile up on the table. Open it, put the bills that need paying in one pile, the items that need attending to (renewals, phone calls, etc.) in another pile and the envelopes and junk mail in the trash. Right away.

Look through your fridge at least once a week and toss out any food that's past its expiration date. Toss out leftovers that are more than three days old. (If you don't like the look of it when it's three days old, you're really not going to like it when it's seven days old.)

In short, de-clutter your life. It's freeing. It reduces stress. You'll have fewer things to dust. And it makes room for the things that are really important to you.

*Calendar:* Keep a calendar. Whether it's on your phone or computer or it's the old-fashioned hang-on-the-wall version, it'll keep you on time, stop you from standing people up, and enhance your reputation for reliability. I love glancing at my wall calendar every Monday to see what the week holds. And I glance at it again every morning to see what the day holds. Anyone in the household can glance at it at anytime to see what's coming up in the next day, month or year. My husband will be talking to someone and say to me, "are we free for dinner on Friday night?" and I'll say, "let me check the calendar" (or I might suggest with just a touch of snark, "why don't you check the calendar?"). I put everything on the calendar—birthdays, appointments, important events, training stats, flight info, etc. Then at the end of the year when I get a new calendar for the new year and I'm transferring birthdays, I get to relive the whole year, like a life review. It's kind of cool.

*Lists:* I believe in lists. Grocery lists. To-do lists. Business idea lists. Books to read lists. And the list goes on (get it?). For me, writing something down releases the anxiety that goes along with trying to remember it. How often do you think to yourself, "now what was that thing I needed to buy" . . . or "person I was going to call" or "thing I was supposed to do"? Lists make your life simpler and more efficient. They help to prevent that second shopping trip due to a forgotten item. They save you time. Apple wouldn't have included a List App on all of their devices if they weren't useful.

*"You are free to choose, but you are not free to alter the consequences of your decisions."*

- *Ezra Taft Benson*

# 10 SAFETY

Moving out and living on your own for the first time can be kind of scary. You won't have a parent there making sure the doors are locked against intruders and the stove is turned off so you don't start the house on fire. If you'll be living alone, the sounds you hear in the middle of the night will be a little unsettling at first. Being aware and being prepared will help you go out on your own with confidence.

**Random Safety Tips:**

Don't open your door to strangers. My daughter was living in LA (Hollywood Blvd, no less) when she heard a knock on the door. Without looking out the window first to see who it was, she opened the door only to see an obviously deranged man on her porch. He nearly made it into the apartment before she got the door closed again. The police arrived moments later because some neighbors from down the road had already called in a complaint. But it could have been worse. It was a good lesson for her to always look before unlocking.

Do you have GPS in your car? Don't set a destination that says 'home' on your GPS. If your car is stolen, the thief can simply press your home destination and be taken directly to your house where, chances are, he now has either your house keys (on the car keychain) or your garage door opener to gain access to your home and steal the rest of your stuff too.

Keep your phone and a flashlight on your bedside table. My daughter also keeps mace handy in the event of an unwanted nighttime intruder. Here's something you might not have thought of in an emergency—keep your car keys near your bed and press the car alarm button if you're in trouble. It's loud. It'll attract attention. That's a good thing.

To stop intruders from coming in through windows or patio doors, put a dowel or broom handle in the window track. You can adjust the length of the rod so that you can leave the window open for ventilation, if desired.

## Hazards (electrical shocks, fire, and natural gas leaks):

*Electrical:* The main hazards of electricity are shocks or fire. Shock is caused when the body becomes part of the electrical circuit. Water is a great conductor of electricity, so stay away from water when using electrical devices. Always dry your hands before touching any electrical devices. Never submerge an electrical device unless it's unplugged (and even then, it will most likely ruin it unless it specifically says it is waterproof). Metal is another great conductor so never stick a fork in a toaster to get that stuck piece of toast out (unless you unplug it first). When in doubt, unplug first.[xii]

*Fire:* To avoid sparks and the possible resulting electrical fire, check for frayed cords and bent prongs on a plug. Keep the use of extension cords to a minimum (NEVER plug a major appliance into an extension cord), and don't overload an outlet. Use the correct wattage bulb in lamps and never throw something over the bulb or lamp. The same goes for space heaters—keep them well away from any clutter, clothes, blankets, etc. that could heat up and catch fire. Know where the circuit breakers are in your home. If a breaker is constantly being flipped, chances are there's a problem with that circuit and an electrician should be called in to take a look. Empty your lint screen on your dryer frequently (preferably before every load)—a full lint screen can cause a fire. When pumping gas, turn off your car, put down your cell phone, and don't climb in and out of the car—any spark can ignite gas fumes, even a static charge from sliding into your car seat. Never, ever smoke or light a match near gas pumps.

*Natural Gas:* The main hazard of natural gas is a leak. There are several ways to detect a gas leak, but the most common is smell. Gas has no smell naturally, but a distinctive odor is added to it to help with detection. If you have a gas stove, gas dryer, or a gas water heater in your home, familiarize yourself with the smell of natural gas. If you smell gas, don't turn anything on or off. Don't do anything that could cause a spark (definitely DO NOT light a match or candle!!!). Open some windows, call the gas company and leave the home or the area until it is declared safe by a professional.

## Storms (lightning, tornadoes, hurricanes, earthquakes):

Always respect the power of nature.

*Lightning* strikes the US about 25 million times a year and kills 25-50 people every year in the US (according to the National Weather Service). The saying is, "when lightning roars, get indoors". If you can hear thunder, lightning can strike you. It has a long reach, so don't assume just because the storm cloud is not directly overhead that you are safe. That is especially true if you are in the water (pool, lake, ocean, whatever). Get out of the water as soon as you hear thunder. Believe it or not, even indoors, there is still a threat from lightning. Stay away from electrical equipment, cords, and plumbing, as they are all good conductors if lightning were to hit your house. You should also stay off of porches and away from windows. My dad, a science teacher, would never let us take a shower or use the toilet during a lightning storm and we'd always roll our eyes thinking he was being overly cautious.

But, as an adult who lived in Florida (where thunderstorms occur regularly all summer long), I learned that my dad was right. You can learn more about lightning safety at http://www.lightningsafety.noaa.gov.[xiii]

*Tornadoes* are unpredictable and can develop with very short notice. Even though tornadoes occur most often in the plains states, every state has had a tornado at some time or another. If you hear that there is a Tornado Watch, it means that conditions are right for the formation of a tornado. You should stay alert until the watch has been cancelled. A Tornado Warning means that a tornado has been sighted in the area and that you should take cover, preferably in a basement or cellar. If that is not possible, then go to the lowest level of the building you are in, to an interior room, and away from all windows and exterior doors. If you get caught outside during a tornado, look for a ditch or depression and lie down with your hands over your head to protect yourself from flying debris. If you are driving in a vehicle and see a tornado, stop the car, get out, and find a safe place (building or ditch) until the storm passes.[xiv]

*Hurricanes* are a fact of life if you live near the Gulf of Mexico or the Atlantic Ocean. Hurricane season starts June 1st and ends November 30th. Hurricanes can be tracked and warnings usually begin well before any action on your part is required (a week or more). If a hurricane is expected to head to an area near you, you will have plenty of time to prepare. Preparation will depend on the strength of the hurricane.

Hurricanes are rated according to wind speed: Category 1--winds from 74-95; Category 2--winds from 96-110; Category 3--winds from 111-130; Category 4--winds from 131-155; and Category 5--winds over 155. Always evacuate if told to do so. Sometimes evacuation is as much about flooding as it is about wind. When evacuating, the goal is to get out of the path of the hurricane. If that is not possible or feasible, then at least get out of the flood zone and into a sturdy (brick) building, preferably one with a generator in case the electricity goes out. If the storm is only rated a Tropical Storm or a Category 1 hurricane, you may decide to stay home and weather the storm. If so, get ready for a longer haul than the hit-and-run action of a tornado. Hurricanes move much more slowly and can even stall over an area for days. Most likely the electricity will go out so make sure you have supplies on hand such as those listed below under 'emergency supplies'. Hurricanes can travel across land (although they usually lose their force along the way) or can spawn tornadoes, so just because you don't live in a Gulf or Atlantic state doesn't mean you shouldn't be aware of the proper precautions.

Here's a little hurricane trivia (because I had always wondered and thought you might too). Hurricanes, typhoons and cyclones are all under the larger category of Tropical Cyclones. Only storms that form over the Atlantic and eastern Pacific are called hurricanes. Storms that form north of the equator spin counterclockwise whereas storms that form south of the equator spin clockwise. The difference is due to the earth's rotation on its axis.[xv]

*Earthquakes.* Most of us think of earthquakes as a California problem and especially worrisome in those areas along the San Andreas Fault. But all states are at some risk for earthquakes. Earthquakes are unpredictable and you'll receive no advance warning for them. Most injuries during an earthquake are not caused by the moving ground itself, but by falling objects or collapsing structures. If you are indoors when an earthquake hits, drop to your hands and knees and cover your head to protect yourself from falling debris. Or better yet, crawl under a sturdy desk or table or over to an interior wall or corner. If you're in bed when the quake hits, stay in bed and cover your head with your pillow. Stay away from glass, windows, and anything that could fall on you. If you are outside, stay away from buildings, streetlights, and utility wires. If you are in your car, stop as soon as you can (but not under trees, overpasses or utility wires) and stay in your vehicle for protection against falling debris.

## Emergency Supplies:

I believe that every household should have enough emergency supplies to last at least one week without electricity or access to stores. Electrical outages can occur anywhere and for a variety of reasons (snow or ice storms, hurricanes, tornadoes, earthquakes, human error, terrorism, electrical grid sabotage, EMPs, solar flares, etc., etc.) and although most of the time repairs are made rather quickly, it has been known to take five days or more to reinstate service depending on the severity of the problem and how large of an area was affected in the outage.

*Essential items:*

Water (for drinking and for washing—plan for one gallon/person/day)

Food—canned or non-perishable. Eat food out of the refrigerator first, then the freezer, and then the non-perishables.

Can opener (or opening every can is going to be a major ordeal)

Candles and/or flashlights or both

Lighters or matches or both


*Non Essentials (but things that'll come in handy):*

AM/FM battery-operated radio and extra batteries

Outdoor grill and, if propane, extra tanks/bottles of propane

Cash, in small bills (ATMs and cash registers won't be working)

First aid kit

*"Enjoy the little things in life for one day you'll look back and realize they were the big things."*

\- *Kurt Vonnegut*

# 11 LAST WORDS OF WISDOM

As young adults we like to think we know everything. But learning comes from living and there's a first time for everything. This book is to help fill in the gaps about information you haven't yet been taught or haven't yet experienced in your own life.

Enjoy your new freedom and independence. You are going to make mistakes but that is when you'll learn the biggest lessons. Bad things happen to everyone. Your true character comes out during times of adversity. Pick yourself up and vow to do better the next time.

Remember that it's okay to have fun and let loose, but not at the expense of others.

Aim to be a productive member of society and a positive representative of your generation.

Recycle, vote, apologize, volunteer, join in, be tolerant, try new things, appreciate nature, and laugh—a lot.

# BIBLIOGRAPHY

i My Apartment Map, "Apartment Rental Data: Statistics and Trends on Apartments for Rent," < http://www.myapartmentmap.com/rental_data/>, (accessed January 26, 2015).

ii DebitSavvy, "Using Your Debit Card Safely," 2012, < http://www.debitsavvy.org/debitsavvy-lifestyle/protect-yourself/using-your-debit-card-safely/> (accessed November 2, 2014).

iii About Money, "Will a Bank Overdraft Hurt my Credit Score?" 2015 < http://credit.about.com/od/creditscorefaq/f/will-overdraft-hurt-credit-score.htm> (accessed September 5, 2014).

iv MyFico, "What's in my FICO Scores?" < http://www.myfico.com/CreditEducation/WhatsInYourScore.aspx> (accessed September 5, 2014).

v Richard Russell, "Rich Man, Poor Man (The Power of Compounding)," 2011, < http://www.lewrockwell.com/2011/02/richard-russell/rich-man-poor-man-the-power-of-compounding/> (accessed December 30, 2014).

vi Cars Direct, "Auto Insurance Explained for Dummies," 2013, < http://www.carsdirect.com/car-insurance/auto-insurance-explained-for-dummies>, (accessed August 24, 2014).

vii Progressive Insurance, "Car Insurance Terms and Definitions," < http://www.progressive.com/glossary/>, (accessed August 24, 2014).

viii viii Prof. David J Hanson, Ph.D., "Driving while Texting Six Times More Dangerous than Driving while Drunk," < http://www2.potsdam.edu/alcohol/files/Driving-while-Texting-Six-Times-More-Dangerous-than-Driving-while-Drunk.html#.VMb1rFqTpgA>, (accessed January 20, 2015).

ix Montana Seat Belt Work Group, "Seat Belt Safety: Ideas, Perceptions, and the Facts," < http://www.mdt.mt.gov/safety/docs/seat-belt-facts.pdf>, (accessed January 24, 2015).

x Mayo Clinic, "Sexually transmitted diseases (STDs)," < http://www.mayoclinic.org/diseases-conditions/sexually-transmitted-diseases-stds/basics/prevention/con-20034128>, (accessed August 30, 2014).

xi WebMD, "Understanding Sexually Transmitted Disease Prevention, 2013, < http://www.webmd.com/sex-relationships/understanding-stds-prevention> (accessed August 31, 2014).

xii NFPA, "Electrical Safety Tips," 2014, < http://www.nfpa.org/safety-information/forconsumers/causes/electrical/electrical-safety-in-the-home/electrical-safety-tips> (accessed October 29, 2014).

xiii National Oceanic and Atmospheric Association, "NOAA Knows . . . Lightning,"
http://www.lightningsafety.noaa.gov/resources/lightning3_05 0714.pdf (accessed October 2014).

xiv Roger Edwards, "Tornado Safety," <
http://www.spc.noaa.gov/faq/tornado/safety.html>,
(accessed October 20, 2014).

xv NASA, "How Do Hurricanes Form," March 8, 2012,
<http://spaceplace.nasa.gov/hurricanes/en/>, (accessed October, 2014).

Made in the USA
Middletown, DE
12 December 2018